LEONARDO BOFF

The Lord's Prayer

The Prayer of Integral Liberation

Translated from the Portuguese by
Theodore Morrow

DOVE COMMUNICATIONS
MELBOURNE, AUSTRALIA

ORBIS BOOKS
Maryknoll, New York 10545

Second Printing, March 1985

The Catholic Foreign Mission Society of America (Maryknoll) recruits and trains people for overseas missionary service. Through Orbis Books Maryknoll aims to foster the international dialogue that is essential to mission. The books published, however, reflect the opinions of their authors and are not meant to represent the official position of the society.

First published as *O pai-nosso: a oração da libertação integral*, copyright © 1979 by Editora Vozes Ltda, Rua Frei Luís, 100, 25.600 Petrópolis RJ, Brazil.

English translation copyright © 1983 by Orbis Books, Maryknoll, NY 10545

Manuscript Editor: William E. Jerman

Published in Australia by Dove Communications,
60-64 Railway Road, Blackburn, Victoria 3130

National Library of Australia card number and ISBN 0 85924 237 4

Library of Congress Cataloging in Publication Data

Boff, Leonardo.
    The Lord's Prayer.

    Translation of: O Pai-Nosso.
    Bibliography: p.
    Includes index.
    1. Lord's prayer.   I. Title.
BV230.B63313   1983   226'9606   82-18811
ISBN 0-88344-299-X (pbk.)

Contents

I

The Prayer of Integral Liberation

A spiritual teacher once said:
"If I have no love or I fail to act justly, then inevitably I separate myself from you, O my God, and my worship is nothing but idolatry.

"To believe in you, I must believe in love and believe in justice, and it is much more important to believe in these things than to pronounce your name.

"Without love and justice it is impossible for anyone, at any time, to be in contact with you.

"But those who take love and justice as their guide are on the true path that leads to you."

The incarnation is more than just one of the central mysteries of the Christian faith. It also opens the way to a new understanding of reality: the incarnation signifies the mutual presence of the divine and the human, the compenetration of the historical and the eternal. Each of these dimensions maintains its own identity, and at the same time it enters into the composition of another, a new, reality.

Jesus Christ, who was man and God at the same time, constituted the reality of a paradigmatic and supreme incarnation. To understand this singular novelty, it is not enough to use the categories of transcendence and immanence—the two key factors of

Greek thought. These two categories capture the element of *difference* between the two dimensions—the human is not divine and the divine is not human—but they do not succeed in explaining their coexistence and joint inclusion in one and the same being.

We must have recourse to another category—that of transparency. This category undertakes to manifest the presence of transcendence within immanence, making each transparent to the other. It is in the human that the divine finds realization; the divine transfigures the human. What is most important is the fact that a new reality has appeared, a reality that is unified but in tension, because it is composed of two "others" of differing nature.[1]

THE LAW OF INCARNATION

Christianity can be understood as a prolongation of God's incarnation process. Just as the Son took everything upon himself in order to liberate everything, so the Christian faith seeks to become incarnate in everything in order to transfigure everything. It is in this sense that we say: everything belongs in some way to the kingdom of God, because everything is objectively connected with God and is called to belong to the reality of God's kingdom. Thus the Christian faith is not just interested in those realities described as spiritual and supernatural. It also places a value on the material and the historical. All of these pertain to one and the same schema of incarnation by which the divine penetrates the human and the human enters into the divine.

Against the background of this understanding, the Christian community commits itself to the *integral* liberation of human beings, not just of their spiritual dimension. Even their corporality (and here we refer to the economic, social, political, and cultural infrastructure in their fullest sense) is "called" to absolute realization in God and to become a part of the kingdom of the Father. As a consequence, the Christian community, especially in recent years, has committed itself more and more to the liberation of the oppressed, to those condemned "to remain at the margin of life, experiencing hunger, chronic illnesses, illiteracy, poverty. . . ."

The church, as Pope Paul VI stated and as was reaffirmed at Puebla, "has the duty to proclaim the liberation of millions of human beings, among whom are many of the church's own children; the duty to help bring this liberation forth in the world, to bear witness to it and make sure it is total. None of this is alien to evangelization" (*Puebla* 26; *Evangelii Nuntiandi [EN]* 30).[2] The church involves itself in this temporal endeavor because it is aware that what is temporal is to be penetrated by grace and by the full reality of the kingdom of God. The temporal is to become transparent and sacramental. Well has the poet said: "O street cleaner, as you sweep the streets, you are sweeping the kingdom of heaven" (D. Marcos Barbosa).

NEITHER THEOLOGISM NOR SECULARISM

Two dangers have been called to our attention by Pope Paul VI in *Evangelii Nuntiandi* (1975) and by the bishops at Puebla (1979). The first is that of religious reductionism (theologism). It limits the activities of the Christian faith and the church to a strictly religious sphere—to worship, piety, and doctrine. Pope Paul VI clearly maintained that "the Church is not willing to restrict its mission only to the religious field and dissociate itself from man's temporal problems" (*EN* 34). The Puebla conference states this even more bluntly: "Christianity is supposed to evangelize the whole of human life, including the political dimension. So the Church criticizes those who would restrict the scope of faith to personal or family life; who would exclude the professional, economic, social, and political orders as if sin, love, prayer, and pardon had no relevance in them" (*Puebla* 515).

What is emphasized here is the need to understand Christianity not as *an area* of reality (the religious field) but precisely as a process by which all of reality is incarnated in order to redeem it and make it a part of the kingdom of God. It is important for the Christian faith to be genuine and salvific. And it is salvific, and consequently genuine, when it is in the form of love. And the love that brings us to the threshold of salvation is not a theory, but a practice. Only faith that is compatible with the practice of love is worthy of the name. Its purpose is to integrate the Christian faith with the other realities of life.

The second danger is that of political reductionism (secularism). It restricts the relevance of the Christian faith and of the church to a strictly political area. This would be to reduce the church's mission "to the dimensions of a purely temporal project; its aims would be reduced to a man-centered goal; the salvation of which it is the messenger would be reduced to material well-being. Its activity, forgetful of all spiritual and religious preoccupation, would become initiatives of the political or social order" (*EN* 32; cf. *Puebla* 483).

The Christian faith has a dimension that is oriented toward society, but this dimension does not exhaust it. In its original meaning, its view is oriented to eternity, and from there it contemplates political activity and informs social action. From a point within history it proclaims and calls attention to a salvation that history itself cannot bring forth, a liberation so complete that it creates perfect freedom—and this has already begun here on earth.

These two reductionisms disrupt the transparency and unity of the incarnation process. The essential thing is to overcome this antithetical dualism and to establish a proper integration and an adequate way of relating human liberation to salvation in Jesus Christ (see *EN* 35; *Puebla* 485): "The Church strives always to insert the Christian struggle for liberation in the universal plan of salvation which it proclaims" (*EN* 38; cf. *Puebla* 483).[3]

The postulate of history and of the Christian faith is one of seeking a complete liberation, one that embraces every dimension of human life: physical and spiritual, personal and collective, historical and transcendent. No reductionism, whether it be spiritual or material in orientation, will do justice to the unity of humankind, to the unique design of the Creator, and to the central reality of Jesus' proclamation of the kingdom of God, which embraces creation as a whole.

THE LORD'S PRAYER IN ITS ARTICULATION

In the Lord's Prayer we encounter in a practical way the correct relationship between God and humankind, between heaven and earth, between the religious and the political, while maintaining unity throughout. The first part speaks on God's behalf: the Father, keeping his name holy, his kingdom, his holy will. The second part is concerned with human interests: our daily bread, forgiveness, ever-present temptation, and ever-threatening evil.

The two parts constitute the one prayer of Jesus. God is not just interested in what belongs to him: his name, his kingdom, his divine will. He is also concerned about our affairs: bread, forgiveness, temptation, evil. Likewise we are not just concerned with what is vital to us: bread, forgiveness, temptation, evil. We are also open to the Father's concerns: sanctification of God's name, the coming of God's kingdom, the realization of God's will.

In the prayer of Jesus, God's concerns are not alien to those of human beings, and their concerns are not foreign to his. The impulse by which humankind is directed upward to heaven and supplicates God rebounds back to the earth and exerts its influence on earthly concerns. It is all one movement, enveloped in a profound unity. It is precisely this mutual involvement that generates the transparency to be found in the Lord's Prayer.

What God unifies—our preoccupation with him and our preoccupation with our own needs—let no one put asunder. God should never be betrayed for the sake of earthly needs; at the same time, it will never be legitimate to anathematize the limitations of our earthly existence because of the grandeur one finds in the reality of God. The two together constitute the material of prayer, supplication and praise. This is why we regard the Lord's Prayer as the prayer of integral liberation.

The reality encompassed in the Lord's Prayer is not a pretty picture but one of heavy conflict. Here the kingdom of God confronts the kingdom of Satan. The Father is near (he is our Father) but he is also remote (in heaven). Blasphemies are spoken in this world, which imposes on us the duty to sanctify God's name. The world is ruled by all sorts of evils that exacerbate our longing for the coming of God's kingdom, which is one of justice, love, and peace. The will of God is being violated, and we must give it concrete expression in our conduct. We pray for daily bread because there are many who do not have it. We ask that God forgive us our violations of fellowship, so that we can forgive those who have offended us. We pray for strength in temptations, because otherwise we would fail miserably. We cry out to be set free from evil, because otherwise we would turn our backs on the faith forever. And in the midst of all this conflict the Lord's Prayer preserves an aura of joyful confidence and serene commitment, inasmuch as all of this is integrated into our encounter with the Father.

If we observe closely, we find that the Lord's Prayer deals with the major themes of the personal and social existence of all humankind in every era. There is no reference here to the church, not even a word about Jesus, his death, or his resurrection. God is at the center of the stage, where the other center—that of humanity and its needs—converges. Here we have what is essential. All the rest is corollary or commentary; it is appended to the essential. "Ask great things of God, and he will give you the small ones as well": this is a saying attributed to Jesus by a non-New Testament source, Clement of Alexandria (140–211 A.D.).[4] An important lesson has been preserved for us here: we must open our minds beyond our self-imposed horizons and widen our hearts beyond our self-imposed limits. Then we will find what is essential, so well translated by Jesus into the prayer that he taught us, the Lord's Prayer.

The *order* in which the petitions appear is not arbitrary. They begin with God and only then pass to us. It is in starting with God, from his vantage point, that we become concerned with our own needs. And in the midst of our sufferings we must be concerned with God. Suffering in heaven is connected with suffering on earth.

Any genuine liberation, from the Christian standpoint, starts with a deep encounter with God that moves us to committed action. It is here that we hear his voice as he tells us continually: Go! And, at the same time, any radical commitment to justice and love of others moves us back to God as the true Justice and supreme Love. Here also we hear his voice as he tells us: Come! Any liberation process that does not succeed in identifying the prime mover of every activity, which is God, does not achieve its purpose and does not reach completion. It is in the Lord's Prayer that we encounter this felicitous relationship. There are good reasons why the essence of Jesus' message—the Lord's Prayer—was not formulated as a doctrinal statement but as a prayer.

Our theological and spiritual meditation on the Lord's Prayer seeks to examine and integrate three levels of interpretation. The first level is that of the historical Jesus: What meaning did Jesus himself attribute to the words he spoke? What meaning does his prayer have? From earliest times the Lord's Prayer has been a kind of summary of the message of Jesus. In the form of a prayer it expresses his most radical and profound experience. At this first level we must take care to make use of the most certain findings of exegesis.

The second level of interpretation grows out of an examination of the theology of the apostolic church. The Lord's Prayer has been incorporated into the Gospels of Matthew and Luke in the context of a community prayer. Christians prayed the Lord's Prayer at all their meetings. They assigned a particular meaning to the words in relation to their own life context. It is reflected in the way they edited the gospels and in the theological accents that they imparted to the words of Jesus. Here we must seek to understand the Lord's Prayer in the light of the general theology of the New Testament.

Finally, we will seek to interpret the Lord's Prayer as we hear it in our own day. When we recite the Lord's Prayer today, we inevitably read into it the concerns of our own faith community. Today's Christian community seeks to live and reflect upon the Christian faith in its liberating dimension, in view of the enormous social inequities to which our brothers and sisters are subject. We experience the Lord's Prayer as the perfect prayer of integral liberation.

There are classical commentaries on the Lord's Prayer by the church fathers, such as those by Tertullian (c. 160–225), St. Cyprian (200–258), Origen (185–253), St. Cyril of Jerusalem (died 386), St. Gregory of Nyssa (died 394), St. Ambrose of Milan (339–397), Theodore of Mopsuestia (died 428), St. Augustine (354–430), and St. Francis of Assisi (1181–1226).[5] When we study them, we realize that their authors attach to their commentary on the Lord's Prayer a commentary on their own life, complete with the aspirations and anxieties typical of their times.

There is nothing more natural: to read means to *re*read. If we are to gain any meaning out of the past, we must energize it in terms of the present.

With an awareness of these processes, which are part of any learning experience, we accept the goal and the limitations of our own commentary, located as it is within this situation of our own, so characterized by oppression and by the longing for total liberation. Reciting the Lord's Prayer means evoking the words of his day and recalling the realities of our own. And, surprisingly, we discover ourselves to be the neighbors and contemporaries of Jesus Christ.

II

Praying the Lord's Prayer
with Real Meaning

Our neighborhood has a high concentration of migrants. They came from their own locality in search of a better life, or even for a way to make any kind of living. And they work, they work hard, when they can find employment. They work, but their hands are still empty. The difference is that they make more money for their employers here.

How do they survive? First, they spend as little as possible. They eat beans and, when available, rice, cereal, and eggs. Sometimes a little chicken; any other kind of meat almost never. Clothes and shoes are things they buy on rare occasions. Major purchases are seldom made, and payments are by installment. Even then, there is nothing. They have to work harder. And the whole family goes to work: father, mother, children. The young generation grows up hit or miss, with no care and no affection.

Living here is difficult. Real home life is almost nonexistent. Residents hole up where they can, in apartments and shacks. There are five persons to a room and two families to a shack. Living as they do, piled on top of each other, there is no place to throw their garbage. The water supply comes from the creek where the sewage goes. All the water is contaminated. Who could be healthy under such circumstances? They work hard, eat little, live like animals, and put up with all this filth. Who could stand it? They are subject to all the diseases of the poor: worms, malnu-trition, dehydration, tuberculosis, bronchial pneumonia, menin-gitis. One disease is added to another and the net result is a short lifespan.

We are just an aggregation of scattered organisms; we are not a people. There is no social life for us. There is no help for our economic needs. There is no one to fight for our wages, control the escalating prices, or inspect the spoiled produce. This is reality for us: hard, ugly, and dreary.

—Report of the Santa Margarida basic ecclesial community,
on the outskirts of São Paulo,
published in SEDOC *11 (1978): 345–48*

Prayer is not the first thing that a person does. Before praying, one experiences an existential shock. Only then does prayer pour forth, whether in the form of supplication, or of an act of thanksgiving, or of worship.[6]

It is no different with the prayer that Jesus taught us to pray, the Lord's Prayer. This prayer can be understood only from the context of Jesus' own profound experience, an experience translated into his words and his deeds. In fact, the Lord's Prayer—as Tertullian, a third-century commentator, wrote—is a summary of the whole gospel *(breviarium totius evangelii).*[7] What "existential shock" underlies the Lord's Prayer and the good news of Jesus?

THE WORLD'S OPEN VEINS:
A GROANING CREATION (ROM. 8:22)

As we look around us we are struck by a blatant paradox: alongside the unquestionable goodness, beauty, and grace that are found everywhere, we stumble over the undeniable evil, broken-ness, and perversity that corrupt humankind and its world. Suf-fering is a stumbling block to us. Reality is a tragic thing, bringing tears to our eyes. Humanity is aggressive; its fundamental law is "my life or yours." Catastrophes, elemental convulsions, and dis-orders of cosmic dimensions are a threat to any equilibrium that might be achieved.

The world bleeds from every vein; the blood flows freely. "The whole created universe groans in all its parts as if in the pangs of childbirth," says St. Paul (Rom. 8:22). Creation is not its own master but has been made subject to diabolical forces. Not even in our wildest fantasies do we behold societies where there are no martyrologies, no massacres, no collective crimes. We cannot find creation beneath the rainbow of God's peace; idols rise up everywhere, demanding our worship and seeking to supplant the true and living God.

MISERABLE CREATURE THAT I AM, WHO IS THERE TO RESCUE ME . . . ? (ROM. 7:24)

The contradiction experienced at the human level is even more dreadful. The cry of Job ascends to heaven from one generation to the next, and every ear hears its cry. Everyone can understand how relationships with the world, with work, with other persons, with love, and with justice, have come to be severed. This scission cuts across not only social structures but the human heart as well: "The good which I want to do, I fail to do; but what I do is the wrong which is against my will" (Rom. 7:20).

The urge to dominate is never satisfied, the instinct for destruction is never exhausted, and the number of sacrificial victims is never enough. Not even daily life can escape the shadows cast by the absurd, the enigmatic, and the cruelty of life. The final chapter to the history of pain has not been written.

Not even the Son of Man was spared "loud cries and tears" (Heb. 5:7), anguish (Luke 22:44), and learning "in the school of suffering" (Heb. 5:8). We hear the cry he raises to heaven, expressing his abandonment by God: "My God, my God, why hast thou forsaken me" (Mark 15:34). Paul's exclamatory question captures the heaviness of human tragedy: "Miserable creature that I am, who is there to rescue me . . . ?"

THE CREATED UNIVERSE: WAITING WITH EAGER EXPECTATION (ROM. 8:19)

In confronting this macabre situation there are three attitudes we can adopt: revolt, resignation, or hope against hope.

Revolt

There are those who revolt against the tragic condition of the world and raise their fists to heaven: God does not exist and has never existed! We have more questions to ask him than he has to ask us! The nerve endings of contemporary humanity are charged with accusations against God.[8] If there is a criminal—some say—who should be brought to the bar of justice, it is God. He is omnipotent, therefore he could save his children, and he does not. He delivers us up to torture and to violent death. He behaves like a criminal.

Others cry: I categorically refuse to accept a creation of God in which innocent creatures must suffer. He is a Moloch who thrives on tears, on mangled bodies, on executions by the sword. Such a God is unacceptable!

He is the father of nobody, said Marcion, a second-century heretic, in expressing his interpretation of God's lack of love and the impossibility of loving him as we view the tragedy of our world. Arnold Toynbee, the famous English historian of modern times, was tormented with "a sour note in the Lord's Prayer." He wrote: "God cannot be good and omnipotent at the same time. These are alternative conceptions of God's nature, and mutually exclusive. We have to choose between them."[9]

Reconciling the existence of God as love with the injustice found in the world has always been a challenge to reason since the times of Job. No matter how much such geniuses as St. Augustine or Leibnitz contrive arguments to exonerate God and explain suffering, the suffering still does not go away. Understanding suffering does not do away with it, just as listening to the recitation of recipes does nothing to dispel hunger.

We can understand Job's bluntness with all the "friends" who tried to explain the meaning of suffering: "You like fools are smearing truth with your falsehoods and stitching a patchwork of lies, one and all. Ah, if you would only be silent and let your silence be your wisdom! . . . But for my part I would speak with the Almighty and am ready to argue with God" (Job 13: 4–5, 3).

Resignation

Then there are those who give way to a *metaphysical* resignation: the ultimate principle of reality is good and evil in coexistence. It is God and the devil at the same time. We are subject to their caprices. The world and humankind are an arena where the contradiction inherent in the Supreme Reality is acted out.

There are those who allow for two principles eternally at war with each other: the principle of Good and the principle of Evil. The solution to the problem is not in overcoming evil but in striving to achieve a balance between good and evil, between integration and disintegration. Humankind must get used to living without hope.

There are others who submit to an *ethico-religious* resignation. In God there is no darkness, only light. Evil is done by human beings; they are not victims of fate or of an irresistible temptation, but agents of a freedom that can be frustrated by their own free will. The story of the fall of the human race (Gen. 3) seeks to emphasize this human responsibility. Human beings are so bogged down in their abuse of freedom that they become prisoners to it; they suffer from their historical inability to create a reasonable and comradely life standard. Persons must cultivate patience with themselves and recognize themselves as sinners.

Ecclesiasticus (Sirach) provides us with the prototype of the ascetical, resigned person. There are no illusions here concerning human life or the future of humankind.[10] He calls out to the reader of every age: "Hold fast to him, never desert him. . . . Bear every hardship that is sent you; be patient under humiliation, whatever the cost" (Sir. 2:3, 4). God will not remain remote and indifferent to the cries of the oppressed; he has decided to set them free (Exod. 3:8). The curses pronounced by the poor are heard by God (Sir. 4:6).

The New Testament portrays God in terms of his solidarity in suffering. The Messiah is the just sufferer, the incarnation of the Servant who "bore our sufferings," who was "tormented and humbled by suffering" (Isa. 53: 3–4 = Matt. 8:17). Because he himself "passed through the test of suffering, he is able to help"

(Heb. 2:18). This solidarity does not eliminate suffering, but creates fellowship among those who suffer, makes resignation bearable and protects against despair, through communion with the one who is greater and stronger who also suffered (Col. 1:24; Rom. 8:17; 1 Peter 4:13). But despite all this, the sores remain open and continue to bleed. Again we say: "Miserable creature that I am, who will rescue me?"

Hope against Hope

And then there are those who hope against hope. They are no less realistic than the others; for them also, the world is a vale of tears. They are always being harassed by personal and historical absurdities. Nonetheless, despite the record of suffering in history, they testify to a sense of triumph. In the climax of development and at the foundation of the world, it is not chaos that reigns but cosmos; not the dissociation of everything but its congregation in love. Creation is not evil because it is creation but because it has been sullied by the irresponsibility of human freedom. And they hope for the full revelation of light that will dispel all the darkness. In the language of the Scriptures they hear promises: "Swords will be beaten into mattocks and spears into pruning-knives; nation shall not lift sword against nation" (Isa. 2:4; Mic. 4:3). "All the boots of trampling soldiers and the garments fouled with blood shall become a burning mass, fuel for fire" (Isa. 9:5), for "he shall judge the poor with justice and defend the humble in the land with equity" (Isa. 11:4), and there will be a reconciliation between humankind and nature and other life forces (Isa. 11:6–9). Finally "they shall never again feel hunger or thirst," or cosmic disturbances (Rev. 7:16), for God will be "a God-with-us, he will wipe every tear from our eyes, and there will be an end to death, and to mourning and crying and pain; for the old order will have passed away" (Rev. 21:3, 4). And then there will be a new heaven and a new earth (Rev. 21:1).

This is the language of utopia and of hope. The world's melancholy experience will always be in contradiction to this liberating vision. But the longing will never die; the fantasy is more real than are the brute facts. Thus there will always be spirits that are immunized against the virus of despair and impotence. The prophets of all ages become the cavalry of hope and rise above the horizon like stars of a better tomorrow.

The solution lies in the future; it is only in hope that we have been saved (Rom. 8:24). The evil times continue, and so does our shame. How long, O Lord?

FOR THOSE WHO DWELL IN THE DARKNESS OF DEATH THERE DAWNED A GREAT LIGHT (MATT. 4:16)

It is against this background that we are to understand the appearance of Jesus and the proclamation of his gospel: "The time has come; the kingdom of God is upon you; repent and believe this good news" (Mark 1:15). God has determined to intervene, to put an end to the diabolical situation, and to inaugurate a new order. He is not just proclaiming a future event. He speaks of the present: "Today, in your very hearing this text has come true" (Luke 4:21). The kingdom of God constitutes the central message of the historical Jesus. He never defined just exactly what this kingdom is. But it is not just a high-sounding word; it brings joy to all the people, it is already in our midst, and its total manifestation is imminent. It modifies the reality of this world, so that the blind see, the lame walk, the dead are raised, and sins are pardoned. The poor, the afflicted, and those who have been denied justice are the primary beneficiaries. The best thing we can do is change our lifestyle and adjust to the new situation. The kingdom does not come mechanically. This is not just some theory to explain the tragedies of the world but is a doing, a changing, a new praxis.

Thus the expression "kingdom of God" is a literary device—a synonym for the proper name of God, which the Jews, out of respect, did not dare to pronounce. In other words, "the Lord shall reign forever" (Exod. 15:18) is a way of saying that God appears as the only Lord of history, restores the order that has been violated, deposes the powerful who have lorded it over others, raises up the humble who have been humiliated, and does away with the last enemy, death (1 Cor. 15:26).

For God to free his creation in this way, human beings must participate, and not just as bystanders; otherwise the kingdom of God would be unhuman and an imposition. As we well know, this world is not that kingdom; as God intervenes and we are converted and likewise act upon the world, it is transformed *in situ* into the kingdom of God. So then, it is both a bestowal and an assignment; a gift and a conquest; a present and a future; a celebration and a promise.[11] Hope is now renewed within tormented hearts: "The people that lived in darkness saw a great light" (Matt. 4:16), and that light is Jesus himself, the kingdom personified. Where he is, the kingdom also breaks in.

The plenary manifestation of the kingdom is very near. Jesus shares the conviction of his contemporaries that the total regeneration of everything is imminent. He is not concerned about the when or the how *(tempora et momenta)*, but is concerned rather with the "watching": we must pay attention because the kingdom will come like a thief.[12] And the kingdom of God is being built in opposition to the kingdom of this world. With Jesus the kingdom bursts forth, but the macabre situation of the world still continues. Thus the basic contradiction between the perversion of creation and the wholeness of the new heaven and new earth continues, at least for a brief time.

The apocalyptic of Jesus' day instilled a profound experience of this tension and sense of expectancy. If one does not understand this apocalyptic horizon, it is difficult to understand the historical Jesus, the abruptness of his proclamation, the hope that he aroused, the urgency of the times that it presupposes, and the radicality of the conversion needed as preparation for the supreme crisis.

Acceptance of this global, grass-roots restructuring of reality, such as is promised with the emergence of the kingdom of God, likewise requires faith. Jesus calls for this explicitly and on many occasions: believe this good news (Mark 1:15; Matt. 17:20). It is not at all obvious that *utopia* ("nowhere") is being transformed into *topia* ("somewhere")—that is, into a flowering reality. The Second Epistle of St. Peter reiterates for us the complaint of Jesus' hearers: "Our fathers have been laid to rest, but still everything continues as it always has been since the world began" (2 Peter 3:4). Is it fair to feed your hearers the promises of dreamers? Is it not more sensible and mature to accept reality with all its contradictions? And yet, there are those who go on hoping despite all the factual evidence. As Job said: "If he would slay me,

I should not hesitate; I should still argue my case to his face" (Job 13:15). The heart cannot be cheated forever. Evidence that this is true is to be seen in the resurrection of Jesus: here we see the emergence of the first unmistakable sign of that new heaven and new earth, as the new Adam comes forth (1 Cor. 15:45). Here is perfect liberation!

INSTRUCTED BY JESUS AND BY THE SPIRIT, WE DARE TO SAY: "ABBA! FATHER!" (GAL. 4:6)

The existential shock, referred to above, constitutes the substratum of the Lord's Prayer, the prayer that Jesus taught the apostles. Here we find a crystallization of the very essence of Jesus' experience and the basic landmarks of his teachings. This experience is concentrated in the awareness that the final catastrophe is imminent;[13] the days of this evil world are numbered. But the message is not that of John the Baptist, one of judgment and punishment; it is the message of joy that comes from the final establishment of the kingdom.

In the interim we live in a time of transition; we find a brief waiting period between the termination of the old and the beginning of the new. It is a time of crisis, of temptations, of decisions. Everything is at stake. What can we cling to? How shall we properly prepare for it?

This is the historical context that provides the framework of the Lord's Prayer. Any reconstruction of the original meaning of Jesus' prayer must start with this emergency-type situation. Let us examine in greater detail the occasion on which it was uttered, its historicity, and its structure.[14]

The Lord's Prayer has been transmitted in two versions: a longer one in Matthew (6:9–13) and a shorter one in Luke (11:2–4). We reproduce the two texts here, in parallel:

Matthew	**Luke**
Our Father in heaven,	Father,[c]
thy name be hallowed;	thy name be hallowed;
thy kingdom come,	thy kingdom come.
thy will be done,	
on earth as in heaven.	

Give us today our daily bread.[a]	Give us each day our daily bread.[d]
Forgive us the wrong we have done,	And forgive us our sins,
as we have forgiven those who have wronged us.	for we too forgive all who have done us wrong.
And do not bring us to the test,	And do not bring us to the test.
but save us from the evil one.[b]	

[a]*or* our bread for the morrow   [c]*or* Our Father in heaven
[b]*or* from evil   [d]*or* our bread for the morrow

Why is it that during the years 75–85 A.D., the time when the two Gospels were put into their present form, the Lord's Prayer was transmitted in two versions? Did Jesus teach two versions on different occasions? The specialists tell us that what the evangelists have transmitted to us is the form found in their respective communities.[15]

Historically speaking, this is not—in its present form—a simple prayer of Jesus that we could retranslate from the original Greek text into the original Aramaic text—that is, into the exact words that Jesus spoke.[16] Rather, this is a prayer of Jesus that has been handed down and assimilated in various forms in the various Christian communities of early times, as the Didache also testifies.[17] The historical formula given by Jesus himself is not accessible to us. We know it only in these two versions.

Which one would be the earlier form, closer to the original? Luke gives a shorter form that contains everything that Matthew says in a more expanded form. According to the laws that govern the transmission of a liturgical text, the respected biblical scholar Joachim Jeremias says: "We know that when a shorter redaction is integrally contained in a longer one, the shorter one should be considered the original."[18] Thus Luke would be closer to the original.

The difference in context between Matthew and Luke helps us to understand the textual differences in the two versions. Both involve a context of prayer. Matthew 6:6–15, where the Lord's Prayer appears, is a catechesis on prayer, probably used with neophytes ("do not pray with the ostentation of the Pharisees, or the wordiness of the gentiles, and forgive if you wish to be forgiven"). We also find a catechesis in Luke 11:1-13, but written in another style. Whereas Matthew's Gospel is slanted to Jews who know how to pray and need only learn how to pray correctly, Luke's teaching is for gentiles who do not pray and must be initiated into a prayer life. Hence Matthew is more liturgical, with a tendency to expand, and Luke has a shorter version, with a tendency to concentrate on the essentials. In both cases we have a poetical format, with rhythm and rhyme: something to be read aloud by a group. Other differences will be discussed when we comment on the individual verses.

The roots of the Lord's Prayer are definitely to be found in Judaism, even though Jesus' prayer is very formal and concise, lacking the more rhetorical style found in the Shemoneh 'Esre (a prayer with "eighteen" benedictions, actually nineteen), the Qaddish (prayers recited at the end of celebrations), and the various types of rabbinical prayers.[19]

Luke's version gives us a glimpse of how the Lord's Prayer originated: "Once, in a certain place, Jesus was at prayer. When he ceased, one of his disciples said, 'Lord, teach us to pray, as John taught his disciples.' He answered, 'When you pray, say, Father . . .' " (Luke 11:1-2). The reference to John (the Baptist) hints at the historical background of the narration. The request, "teach us to pray," is equivalent to saying: "give us a summary of your teaching." We know that all religious groups in Jesus' day had their own form of prayer.[20] The prayer serves the function of a kind of creed that bestows unity and identity on the group. Thus the small group saying the prayer of Jesus felt itself a part of the total eschatological community created by Jesus.[21] Thus we may think of his prayer as summing up the quintessence of his purpose and mission. It makes reference to the Father—the intimately personal invocation of the historical Jesus—the coming of the kingdom, the divine providence that provides the essentials for biological life (bread) and for social life (forgiveness, healing of broken relationships), and the crisis of temptation.

Matthew's version gives a better definition of the significance of the Lord's Prayer as the form of prayer that Jesus stresses—

distinguishing it from other prayer practices—by inserting it in a discourse on other practices of piety: giving alms (6:1-4) and fasting (6:16-18).

When we examine the structure of the Lord's Prayer, we immediately note two movements in opposite directions. One is upward, toward heaven: the Father, his holiness, his kingdom, his will; the other is earthward: bread, forgiveness, temptation, evil. Three optatives are directed heavenward; three petitions are made for the earth. Faith has two eyes: one that looks up to God and contemplates his light; another that is turned toward the earth and discerns the tragedy of darkness. On the one hand we sense the impulse of the inner person (spirit) straining upward (to God); on the other hand we experience the weight of the outer person (the flesh) that bends us downward (to the earth).

All of reality, in its greatness and in its obscurity, lies before God. In the Lord's Prayer both the infinite longing for heaven (Our Father in heaven) and its earthly roots (our daily bread) are offered to God on behalf of the world.

We know that in the primitive church the Lord's Prayer belonged to a "secret discipline"; it was only for those who had been initiated into the Christian mystery. It is in the light of this that we are to understand the introductory liturgical formulas, full of reverence and respect, that were used until quite recent times: "Admonished by your teachings and instructed by divine institution, we dare to say: our Father" (from the Roman Missal, prior to the reforms of Vatican II). The Lord's Prayer confronts us with the "secret" of Jesus communicated to the apostles. The prayer that our Lord taught us cannot be prayed in just any way and with just any attitude. It presupposes a perception of all this world's tragedy; as we suffer in the passion of history, it promises us liberation.

To pray the Lord's Prayer requires an act of faith, hope, and love. In order to pray it, as Tertullian noted, we must profess faith in God as Father despite his silence, his remoteness, and our overwhelming environment of suffering.[22] He is a kind Father. Looking about us at the world, we cannot confirm this, but we believe. It is also an act of hope: may your kingdom come, may your will be done forever! We firmly expect the Father to wipe away all tears and rework the structures of his creation. Then, and only then, will the shalom of God shine upon us. And it is an act of love. We do not just say Father, but *our* Father. Here we find all the warmth and intimacy of love; the word "Abba" that Jesus uses means something like "Dad," "Daddy," "dearest Father"!

Perhaps we may not have the courage to call God by such a familiar name. But the Spirit of Jesus, infused in our hearts, prays on our behalf: Abba, Father (Gal. 4:6; Rom. 8:15). For we recognize ourselves as sons and daughters in his Son because with Jesus we make up the eschatological fellowship and because the Spirit moves us so that we pray: Our Father!

III

Our Father in Heaven

Father,
descend from the heavens, forgive
the prayers that my ancestors taught me,
poor persons who are now at rest,
who could only wash and clean,
who could only be concerned, all day long,
with what they could wear,
who could only spend the nights in watching, painfully,
praying, asking you for things,
softly murmuring their complaints.

Descend from the heavens if you exist, descend,
for I am dying of hunger in this little corner,
not knowing why I had to be born,
looking upon my swollen hands,
having no work, having nothing;
come down a bit, and look at
this broken shoe,
this anguish, this empty stomach,
this city that has no bread for my mouth,
the fever that eats at my flesh,
thus to fall asleep,
under the rain, tortured by the cold, persecuted.

22

I tell you that I do not understand, Father,
come down, touch my soul,
look upon my heart,
I am not a robber or an assassin, I am a child,
and for that they give me blow after blow;
I tell you that I do not understand, Father;
come down, if you exist,
for I seek to be resigned to myself and cannot,
and I am filling up with anger
and preparing myself to do battle,
and crying out until my throat fills with blood,
for I cannot take it any longer, I have feelings
and I am a man.
Come down! What will you do with your creature, Father?
A mad animal who chews the paving stones of the street?
       — "Oração de um desocupado"
       ("Prayer of an Unemployed Man"),
       by Juan Gelman, Argentine poet

In our initial comments on the Lord's Prayer, we attempted to recreate the existential atmosphere that gave birth to the prayer of Jesus. Underlying this is the impression created by the paradox of this world: God's good creation is dominated by the diabolical forces that torment our lives and threaten our hopes. The kingdom of God represents the reversal of this situation; out of the heart of darkness bursts a liberating ray of light. The kingdom is already at hand and is already happening in our midst! A great crisis is being prepared, a final decision is imminent. In the midst of this high pressure and the painful suffering of this world, Jesus teaches us to pray: Our Father in heaven.

As we look at the deformed and deviant course of this world, it is not in the least evident that God is a beloved Father (Abba). We need faith, hope, and love to overcome the temptation to skepticism and revolt, as we repeat with Jesus: Our Father. If he had not taught us this and asked us to pray it, then certainly we never would have dared to call out, with such confidence and intimacy, "Dear Father." We recite the Lord's Prayer and we live it each day, despite all the contradictions, because we are heirs of the inexhaustible source of hope in Jesus, which is opposed to all evidence to the contrary. Because of this hope and this confidence, the darkness is no less dark, but it is less absurd. The dangers have not been removed, but our courage has been strengthened.

We shall develop our reflections at two levels. First of all, we shall seek to enter into the thinking and experience of Jesus.[23] Secondly, we shall attempt to pray the Lord's Prayer in the context of the oppressive forces that weigh down upon contemporary humanity and make its life unhappy.

UNIVERSALITY OF THE EXPERIENCE
OF GOD AS FATHER

The fatherhood of God—the central theme of the kingdom of God as taught by Jesus—has universal roots and reaches the most archaic levels of our internal archeology. Both the old and the new are present in Jesus. On the one hand he adopts what is universally human and brings it to its ultimate culmination. On the other hand he introduces an originality all his own. The utterance, "Dear Father," resonates with one of the most ancient archetypes of all human experience, and at the same time it reveals the unique and intimate relationship that Jesus enjoyed with God.

For the sake of clarity, we shall distinguish three modalities in the use of the expression "father" when applied to God: as designation, as declaration, and as invocation.[24]

A feature of the ABCs of any authentic religious experience is the unthematic perception of an offspring/parent relationship between humanity and divinity. Religious persons see themselves as the image and likeness of their God. They perceive of themselves as children, and they think of God as father or as mother.[25] Primitive peoples, such as the Pygmies, the Australian aborigines, and the Bantu, all the way to the most highly developed peoples of antiquity, such as the Egyptians, Assyrians, Greeks, Romans, and those of the Indus Valley, all designated God as father.[26] This expression is used to translate the idea of absolute dependence on God, and at the same time to denote an inviolable respect and unrestricted trust. Persons give thanks to divinity for their existence and relate to it as a child relates to mother or father, or as a young person relates to one who is older.

In more primitive times the expression "father" was less associated with generation and creation, which implies a material basis for the image and idea of the family. In a more primitive social organization based on groups of elders and groups of younger persons, the expression "father" is a translation of the authority, power, and wisdom of the elders. Thus we are dealing with a designation and title conveying honor.

"Father" then came to mean the creator and generator of everything; the Romans regarded Jupiter and other gods (Mars, Saturn) as *pater, parens, et genitor.*[27] Here divinity appears as universal lord and king. Homer, in his *Iliad*, speaks of the chief Greek divinity: "Zeus, father, you rule over gods and humans."[28] Aristotle, in his *Politics*, declares that the power of the father over his children is like that of a king.[29]

So then, the designation "father" must be understood in the light of these two activities: as generator-creator and as the highest authority and lord, not a sinister or frightening master but one who is approachable and full of kindness. Thus we are to understand the famous Sumerian hymn of Ur, dedicated to the moon god Nanna, which reads: "King, merciful father, in whose hand is the life of the whole earth," or the hymn to Marduk, which reads: "His wrath is like a tempest, and his serenity and kindness are like that of a merciful father."[30] Here we find the same divine qualities that were experienced by Israel: the God as father, possessing absolute authority and infinite mercy.

With reference to Israel and Israel's relation to God as father, there are some specific problems. The Old Testament is slow to represent God as father. There is a basic difficulty that justifies the rare occurrence—only fifteen times—of the name "father" applied to Yahweh.[31] Biblical authors were waging a constant war against the anthropology of the Middle East nations that held that human beings have their origin in a god (or the blood of a god) who was expelled from heaven and died; in other words, they maintained that humans are divine. Biblical faith would not accept this theistic anthropology: it is an indiscriminate mixture of God and humankind, divinizing what dare not be divinized (the creature) and profaning what dare not be profaned (God). This is why the sacred authors tended to avoid the use of a father-son relationship to express the way God relates to humans.[32] But, despite this, the figure of God as Father still emerges from the Old Testament background of Israel's experience of God.

The experiential basis for this is that of a God who takes his place at the side of the fathers of the nation to assist them in their journey (which is the significance of "Yahweh"). Thus he is represented as the "God of our fathers," of Abraham, Isaac, and Jacob. God makes a covenant with his people and gives them the Law as an expression of his covenant and way of holiness. He is a God—and this is unique in the comparative history of religions— who is represented by a name but not an image, with a connotation but with no denotation: "I am who I am." This is the true name of Yahweh, a name that makes no appeal to fantasy, to dream language, or to symbolism, thus nipping in the bud any attempt to establish anthropomorphism and idolatry. "If . . . they ask me your name, what shall I say? God answered: I AM who I am. Tell them that I AM has sent you to them" (Exod. 3:13–14). Thus we conclude that Yahweh was not initially experienced as Father.

By the same token, the experience of having been chosen as a people from among other peoples, whom Yahweh has liberated from Egypt and thus won for himself, allowed Israel to designate God as Father. This designation is allowed only by virtue of its creation as a people. In Exodus, God himself says: "Israel is my firstborn son" (Exod. 4:22). Israel recognizes that it owes its existence as a people to God: "Is he [Yahweh] not your father who formed you? Did he not make you and establish you?" (Deut. 32:6; see also Num. 11:12; Isa. 63:16, 64:8; Mal. 2:10).

This allusion to God as Father is expanded by the prophets. They developed a radical sense of ethics. If God is Father, we owe it to him to behave as submissive, obedient children. But this is not the end of it. God himself, speaking through the prophetic word, declares himself Father: "A son honors his father, and a slave goes in fear of his master. If I am a father, where is the honor due to me? And if I am a master, where is the fear due to me? So says the Lord of hosts" (Mal. 1:6).

The same criticism is found in Jeremiah: "Not so long since, you called me 'Father, dear friend of my youth' " (Jer. 3:4), and yet, God says, "You have played the harlot" (3:1).

Jeremiah depicts God's feelings:

> I said, How gladly would I treat you as a son,
>> giving you a pleasant land,
>>> a patrimony fairer than that of any nation!
> I said, You shall call me Father
>> and never cease to follow me.
> But like a woman who is unfaithful to her lover, so you,
> Israel, were unfaithful to me.
>> This is the very word of the LORD [3:19–20].

As the prophets speak in the name of a repentant people, what emerges is an explicit declaration of God as a compassionate Father:

> Look down from heaven and behold
> from the heights where thou dwellest holy and glorious.
>> Where is thy zeal, thy valor,
>>> thy burning and tender love?
> Stand not aloof; for thou art our father,
> though Abraham does not know us
> nor Israel acknowledge us.
> Thou, LORD, art our father;
>> thy name is our Ransomer from of old
>>> [Isa. 63:15–16; see also Isa. 64:8; Jer. 3:4].

It is Jeremiah who expresses in the name of God the promptness of his paternal pardon: "Is Ephraim still my dear son, a child in whom I delight? As often as I turn my back on him I still remember him; and so my heart yearns for him. I am filled with tenderness toward him. This is the very word of the Lord" (21:20). As may be seen, the paternal relationship of God is so tender and intimate that God emerges not only as father but also as mother (see Isa. 49:15, 66:13). We feel the same caring here as in the home of our parents: "When Israel was a boy, I loved him; I called my son out of Egypt" (Hos. 11:1).

Despite all these impressive passages, the name "father" applied to God is not a definitive one in the Old Testament.[33] It is one name among others, many of which occur more frequently and are of greater importance, such as Lord, King, Judge, Creator. The expression "father" usually occurs in conjunction with the sacred name Yahweh and other names for God. The relationship would seem to apply to the people as a whole and not to any one person in particular.

The invocation of God as "my Father" or "our Father" never occurs directly in any prayer in the Old Testament.[34] The language is always indirect, as though there were a promise that someday was to be fulfilled. "He shall cry to me, Thou art my Father, my God, and the rock of my salvation" (Ps. 89:26). It was for Jesus of Nazareth to introduce this innovation and thus to bring to its profoundest intimacy the religious relationship of the human person finding itself a child as it experiences God as Father.

ORIGINALITY OF JESUS' EXPERIENCE: ABBA

Calling God "Abba" ("dearest father, dad, papa") is one of the most salient characteristics of the historical Jesus. *Abba* belongs to the language of childhood and the home, a diminutive of endearment that was also used by adults for their own fathers and older persons for whom they wished to show respect.[35] It had never entered into anyone's head to use this familiar, commonplace expression to refer to God. That would be failing to show respect to Yahweh and would scandalize godly persons. And yet Jesus, in all his prayers that have come down to us, addressed God with the expression "Dearest Father" (*Abba*). We find this expression in the mouth of Jesus 170 times in the Gospels (4 times in Mark, 15 in Luke, 42 in Matthew, and 109 in John). And the Greek New Testament preserves the Aramaic expression *Abba*, thus retaining this remarkable example of Jesus' audacity (Rom. 8:15; Gal. 4:6).

"Abba" alludes to the secret of Jesus' intimate relationship with God and his mission in the name of God. "Jesus thus spoke with God as a small child speaks with its father—with simplicity, intimacy, confidence."[36]

Of course, Jesus also knew the other names of God found in the tradition of his people. His use of "Abba" in no way detracts from a respectful, serious attitude toward God, as may be seen in many of his parables where God is shown as King, Lord, Judge, and Vindicator. But all of these are subordinate to the great rainbow arc of God's incomparable goodness and tenderness as seen in "Dear Father." All the other titles are *common* nouns or names for God; Father is God's proper name. Jesus has received this revelation from God himself: "Everything has been entrusted to me by my Father; and no one knows . . . the Father but the Son and those to whom the Son may choose to reveal him" (Matt. 11:27).

The eschatological promise made by Yahweh to his people has at last been fulfilled, the promise that is implicit in the tetragram YHWH revealed to Moses: "But on that day my people shall know my name; they shall know that it is I who speak: here am I" (Isa. 52:6).[37] The name Yahweh means "I am here" (it is I who am with you). And what this actually means is now evident as Jesus calls upon God as "Dear Papa." Thus "Abba" signifies "God is in our midst; he comes near us with his mercy, kindness, and tenderness." We entrust ourselves to his care just as a small child confidently and serenely entrusts itself to its father or mother.

Jesus does not invoke God only as *my* dear Father, but also teaches us to invoke him as *our* heavenly Father, with the same confidence that he himself does. It is with this childlike approach that we open the gates of the kingdom of heaven: "Unless you turn around and become like children, you shall never enter the kingdom of Heaven" (Matt. 18:3). And this Father is not just Father of the faithful, as we read in Psalm 103:13 ("As a father has compassion on his children, so has the Lord compassion on all who fear him"), but he is the Father of everyone without discrimination: "He himself is kind to the ungrateful and the wicked" (Luke 6:35) and "causes his sun to rise on the bad as well as the good, and his rain to fall on the honest and the dishonest alike" (Matt. 5:45).

This closeness and intimacy with God that is implied in the expression "Abba" is identical with the "closeness" of the kingdom of God. Thus the name Father applied to God pertains to the content of Jesus' teachings as centralized in the theme of the kingdom.[38] This unrestricted trust in the Father's providence and total abandonment to the cause of the kingdom are not parallel subjects. On the contrary, the confidence that persons achieve by realizing they are in the hands of the Father frees them from the preoccupations of this world, so that they may aspire to the one thing necessary, which is the kingdom of God (Luke 12:29–31). The idea of a provident Father ("your heavenly Father knows that you need" [these things—i.e., food, drink, clothing, etc.]—Matt. 6:32) is incorporated into the more extensive theme of the kingdom of God, which is imminent and has already begun to emerge in the message, deeds, and person of Jesus: "Set your hearts on his kingdom, and these other things will be given you as well" (Luke 12:31). The benevolent goodness of God is now seen in its plenary form: it extends not only to creation ("Are not sparrows two a penny? Yet without your Father's leave not one of them can fall to the ground. As for you, even the hairs of your head have all been counted"—Matt. 10:29–30), but history has now in principle achieved its fulfillment: "Have no fear, little flock, for your Father has chosen to give you the Kingdom" (Luke 12:32).

GOD THE FATHER: NEAR AND YET FAR AWAY

When Christians, at Jesus' prompting, pray the Lord's Prayer, they are not thinking primarily of a creator of a fathomless mystery from which everything else emanates. This idea is not exactly absent, but it is not the catalyst for religious experience. The innovation is to be found in the recovery of what has been experienced by Jesus and transmitted to us through the apostles—namely, that God is here as a Father who cares for his children, that he has a heart that is sensitive to our problems, that his eye is always upon our sufferings, and that his ear is open to our cries. A person is not a digit or subparticle lost in the terrifying infinity of space, but is someone enveloped in the solicitous love of God. We know his name and keep it in our heart. We can trust ourselves to the care of this Father-God. We may abandon both life and death to him, because whatever is happening and will happen is for our good.

Drawing this close to the Father, we can feel that we are his sons and daughters. Here, being a son or daughter is not a causal category (a person biologically descendant from the Father), but mostly a category of personal relationship.[39] The son or daughter is so to the extent that they cultivate both intimacy and trust with respect to the Father. Paul says it very well:

> To prove that you are sons, God has sent into our hearts the Spirit of his Son, crying "Abba! Father!" You are therefore no longer a slave but a son, and if a son, then also by God's own act an heir [Gal. 4:6–7].
>
> The Spirit you have received is not a spirit of slavery leading you back into a life of fear, but a Spirit that makes us sons, enabling us to cry "Abba! Father!" [Rom. 8:5].

Thus a new community is emerging here, one of brothers and sisters in the elder brother, Jesus; all of us are sons and daughters in the Son, and we are encouraged to call out with the same cry as the Son Jesus: Abba!

Having dealt with the vertical dimension of offspring to Father, we now pass to the horizontal dimension of fellowship: we pray together, *Our* Father. No one is an island. We are all involved in the messianic community of the Father's kingdom. The Father of Jesus Christ is not just the Father of *some* persons, but the Father of all, especially the lowly and the poor, in whom he is present (Matt. 25:34–45) and to whom he reveals himself (Matt. 11:25), to those who most frequently must call upon him for their daily bread.

IN HEAVEN

Matthew's version of the prayer is the one that we usually recite: Our Father (who art) in heaven. The phrase "in heaven" has various levels of meaning.[40] One level emphasizes the ubiquitous presence of the Father: he is not tied down to certain sacred places or to one people, one fraction of humankind. His presence is not concentrated in the Temple, or on Mount Zion, or on Sinai, or in the mountains, or in the desert. He is beyond all this, but he is there too, offering his paternal kindness to all.

We see at once that this emphasizes the uniqueness of the Father. He has no rivals, whether by way of fathers of the faith and of the nation, or earthly fathers. On the contrary, every family derives from him (Eph. 3:14–15). As his own Son Jesus has said: "You have one Father, and he is in heaven" (Matt. 23:9).

But there is another, more profound meaning, a theological interpretation: the expression "in heaven" is meant to highlight the remoteness of the Father. He is a Father who is near, by being compassionate and kind, but he is also a quite "other" Father. He is not to be confused with one's earthly father, for he is not a simple extension of the characteristics of one's biological father. He is by our side, and he is not indifferent to our lives or our pains, but he continues to be the totally Other. He "dwells" in heaven.

Heaven, in the oldest human cultures, is a symbol of transcendence, of the infinite that humankind cannot attain by its own efforts. Thus heaven becomes the archetypal symbol of God, the Most High, the God of glory and inaccessible light.

God is near, which is why he is Father, and he is so near that he is *our* Father. But this God is not a mannequin that we have erected as a disguise for the narcissism of our infantile desires for protection and consolation at any price. This God calls upon us to forget ourselves, our own desires and interests, ushering us into the kingdom of meanings that are beyond any earthly good or evil.

Access to the Father-God is not as easy as would seem at first glance. The path is rough and arduous, and requires courage to follow. As we have already said, it requires faith, hope, and love, the ability to bear with the contradictions of this world and, at the same time, to call out: Abba, Father. It calls us to the struggle of transforming this world from the kingdom of Satan to the kingdom of God, thus making the invocation "Our Father" more believable. Only a God who is so near and yet so far could help us find an earthly way of life that leads to heaven. Heaven, not earth, is our homeland.[41]

God, and not this world with its tyrannical structures and historical tragedies, constitutes "the hearth and homeland of human identity." Any "protection" or "care" that the idea of father can generate that is not directed toward this goal must be disqualified theologically in the name of the Father of our Lord Jesus Christ and of Jesus himself. The invocation "Our Father in heaven" basically implies a profound declaration of faith in the fact that God, the near and remote God, is the living and true God who, in defiance of all the mechanisms of death and destruction to which we are subject, is already building his kingdom—a kingdom of love, kindness, and fellowship—in our midst.

HOW SHALL WE PRAY THE LORD'S PRAYER IN A FATHERLESS WORLD?

We want to be aware of any fundamental obstacles that cause difficulty in praying the Lord's Prayer. There are four such obstacles: the seriousness of the crisis in the meaning of life, the emergence of a fatherless society, criticisms leveled at the father-figure and its function in religion by such thinkers as Freud and Nietzsche, and, finally, an awareness of the relativity of our own culture with respect to the father-figure. If we can overcome these obstacles, we shall have cleared a field of faith in which the recitation of the Lord's Prayer will recover its full liberative significance.

Some persons are so struck by the negative features of life that they have lost their hope and faith; they see no meaning in lifting their eyes to heaven and praying the Lord's Prayer. Such a recitation, for them, would not be authentic; in fact, it would be a lie. For them, God is not experienced as a Father. *Fata nos ducunt*, the ancients said: we are led by fate; blind, we are directed by unknown powers.

There are others who have joined in battle against the oppressions of this world and have succumbed to the feeling of impotence when confronted by the gravity of life's absurdities and the historical violence against human dignity and justice. They have lost their faith in the possibility of humankind's recovery and liberation. They say: we are forever condemned to devour one another, subject to the law of "might makes right." Yet they are always tormented by dreams of fellowship, freedom, and equality. Cynicism and despair kill faith. Resignation makes one speechless before God, so that one has only questions that could be asked of God, but no supplications, no invocations.

This is a terrible temptation, and it can come even to religious-minded persons. It can be overcome to the extent that a person succeeds in getting beyond the level of religious emotionalism to walk the path of faith. Religious emotionalism is built on just that: emotion; it comes from a desire for protection and a fear of punishment.[42] It is an age-old structure, tied to the rudiments of our emotional and social life. If God dwelt within this horizon, he would be assimilated only as a Father who protects or a Judge who punishes. God would be deprived of his divinity, to be instrumentalized in line with human needs.

The truth is that there are realities against which we cannot protect ourselves; we have to either resist them or put up with them. God does not pull us out of the perilous waves, but gives us courage. If God existed only to draw us out of the waves and not to give us courage in our crisis, then he would perish or be rejected when our hope died or our existential balance was lost.

We noted above that the Father of our Lord Jesus Christ is not a mere protector God. It is true that he comforts us and has compassion on his children. But he is in heaven, not on earth; this distance is always a fact. Thus he is only *our* Father to the extent that we accept him as the Father in heaven. That is, we have no other access to him except by faith as a decision freely made, establishing an independent filial relationship, not a dependential relationship. Faith prompts us to accept the goodness of God at the same time as we accept the evil in the world. Beyond earth, in heaven, there is meaning for everything, even for the contradiction that tears at our hearts here and now and fills our eyes with tears. God continues to be *our* Father despite the suffering we undergo. Our freely-made decision has already given us victory over the area of religious emotion and has inaugurated the kingdom of faith. Here is the true escape from the slavery of desire for protection into the freedom of living beyond it. It is the exodus from "woe unto you" to the joy of "blessed are you."

This faith is required of us in praying the Lord's Prayer. This faith was manifested by Jesus. He himself confided in God at the most despairing moment of his crucifixion; he was faithful to God despite contradiction, persecution, and condemnation.

We are, as some say, "on the road to a fatherless society."[43] Contemporary cultures are still patriarchal, but they are undergoing a profound crisis. Technological progress makes it impossible to maintain a paternal form of domination. The image of the working father has grown dim; his occupational activities are becoming increasingly less visible to his children. The distance between his residence and his place of work, the social division of labor, and the status of the wage earner have all destroyed his authority. He is reduced to a mere cog in the sophisticated machinery of society. The social order is no longer incarnated in a person—the father—as a symbol and guarantee of public order, but finds its incarnation in officials who perform their functions and then join the ranks with all the others. "Patriarchal society has been replaced by a fatherless society or by a peer society that performs anonymous duties and is directed by impersonal forces."[44] There is nothing deviant about this. It is the ripening of a social process that opens up a new phase in human evolution. Thus it consists in dismissing the father without bearing him any grudge.

In this situation, what does it mean to pray the Lord's Prayer? Does it not mean to perpetuate the parameters of a culture that is now obsolete? Although we are moving more and more into a society with increasingly impersonal, egalitarian ties (and this is what the world wants; it is not just something that we notice), we still cannot concede that the father-figure has been eliminated. We must search out the nuclear model of our patriarchal order, the anthropological principle of paternity. The historical social expression of paternity, as the axis around which a type of society is organized, may vary, but there is an anthropological constant of paternity that is not exhausted by the particular form of social concretization. This factor has an inalienable function, responsible for that first break in the intimacy between mother and child, the introduction of the child into the social milieu. The father-figure is not doomed to disappear, but will take on new roles compatible with a changed world. It continues to be internalized in the psyche of children, becoming a matrix by which they assimilate, reject, and come to terms with the world.[45]

Freud teaches that everyone forms the idea of God out of the image of their father; their relationship to God depends on the relationship they have had with their father. If the human father, as one of the active members of a changed society, has sufficient sincerity, fidelity, and responsibility to guarantee the protection that children need to provide a maturation of their ego, then he may again perform the function of a model—and free of any encumbrances from the patriarchal era. He may again exercise that function within the structuring that is inherent to the father-figure

in human society. This anthropological base serves as a spring-
board for the child to develop its image of God as a fruition of
adult faith, not as a sedative for the instinct of protection. He is a
Father even in the darkness of internal night or the grief over
nameless suffering.

These thoughts help us to understand and resolve another difficulty that is raised by those masters of suspicion, Nietzsche and
Freud.[46] They have posed a number of criticisms of this religion of
the Father, starting with a hermeneutic of evasions and conceal-
ments that have to do with two profound impulses of human existence: desire and fear. The desire for protection and the mechanisms for overcoming fear may create a language under which
they may be hidden—that is, religion. According to these
authors, religion has a significance as an escape for religious persons. They live within an illusion, thinking that they are dealing
with God, his grace, his forgiveness, his protection, and his salvation, whereas in truth they are only taming and channeling their
basic drives. The suspicion of the analyst (such as Freud or
Nietzsche) must be able to detect this concealment, isolate those
conscious, canonized meanings from the unconscious factors.
Thus for Nietzsche religion, especially Christianity, has its origin
in the resentment that the weak bear for the strong, born of impotence and frustration, a kind of "Platonism for the poor." Values
are inverted so that the weak become strong, the impotent become
omnipotent, and God is crucified and defeated.[47]

For Freud, who takes the same line of interpretation, religion is
a collective infantile neurosis, and God is "a projection that com-
pensates for the feeling of infantile helplessness."[48] God the
Father becomes a substitute for one's own father, a projection
and, finally, an illusion by means of which one is sustained by a
feeling of protection and comfort. Persons are set free when they
renounce the principle of pleasure (desire) and adopt the principle
of reality (*amor fati*, acceptance of fate).

Freud insists that everyone passes through the Oedipus com-
plex. The problem is not that one enters it (everyone goes through
it); the problem is how to get out of it in a way that retains one's
humanity and integrates it into one's personal life plan. In its basic
makeup, the Oedipus assumes a root-structure of desire in the
form of megalomania and omnipotence. Desire has no limits.

Thus the Oedipus, in fantasy, is transformed into the image of the ideal father, controller of all the values desired by the son. The son thus imitates his father and is fascinated by him. He wants to be like him. But how can he accomplish this?

There are various ways of getting out of the Oedipus. Repression, identification, and sublimation are unsuccessful approaches and are never totally achieved. One way to emerge from the Oedipus is by a demolition (dissolution or destruction) of the Oedipus. This is accomplished by recognizing that one's father is mortal and that he differs from his son. The son will never be the father. The father must be accepted as a father; this makes the son really a son. This is not a matter, then, of repressing our desires but only of unmasking them, of renouncing the omnipotence they possessed in childhood. The son thus interiorizes the father-figure without denying his own sonship; he himself becomes a father in his own right and achieves maturation as a human being. It is in this way that the Oedipus is once again incorporated, in its integrity, into the psyche.[49]

With the data that we have surveyed on the dialectical structure of the experience of God as near and remote Father, our Father and at the same time the Father who is in heaven, we are ready to respond to the criticisms of Freud and Nietzsche. We have to concede that there is a pathological form of living out this belief in God as Father that is an evasion of the suffering of this world and an insatiable search for consolation. In this case we have to accept the criticism of these two masters of suspicion; they exercise a purifying action on the true faith.

On the other hand, if we look carefully at the matter, we see that the faith required in praying the Lord's Prayer actually seeks to liberate us from the primeval drives of desire and fear that keep us in slavery, that impede us from saying, "Abba, Father" with freedom as adults, rather than with the immaturity of small children. St. Paul insists that we are no longer "during our minority slaves to the elemental spirits of the universe" (Gal. 4:3)—in other words, slaves to desire and fear—but adult offspring. The relationship that we have established with the Father-God does not grow out of an infantile, neurotic dependence but out of autonomy and a freely-made decision.

In Jesus we see this Oedipal integrative attitude clearly shining forth. He does not live with a feeling of emasculation in the presence of his Father, nor is his feeling one of immobilizing dependence. On the contrary, he has his own mission, he sees himself as a son and recognizes the Father as his heavenly Father. He renounces the dream of infantile omnipotence, the urge to usurp the privileges of the Father, thus seeing himself and accepting himself as the Son.[50] On the one hand, he knows that he has received everything from the Father (John 17:7); on the other hand, he knows, through the relationship of intimacy and love that he has with the Father, that he is one with him (John 17:21). This free relationship of the Son-Jesus clears the way for the Father-God to have a relationship with other human beings. Jesus demonstrates a totally free and open relationship, one that loves to the point of sacrificing his life for others. The vertical dimension emerges as a source of power for the horizontal dimension. The liberation of human beings does not conflict with their relationship to God. Jesus demonstrates that he can have profound ties to God and yet be radically bound to men and women; in other words, liberation from human oppression does not necessarily imply liberation from the idea of God as Father.

Thus it becomes clear that Christianity does not have its origin in the resentment of the weak against the strong. It is not the religion of resignation and frustration but of dignity, the courage to keep up the two polarities that have to be maintained—of faithfulness to heaven and faithfulness to the earth, of hope against hope. At its origin, Christianity was a religion of slaves and marginals, but it did not confirm them in their slavery and marginality. It led them to freedom and to the stature of the dignity of a new person.

The fourth difficulty has to do with the historical consciousness of our culture centered on the father-figure and masculine orientations. Could it be that calling upon God as Father means paying tribute to a passing phenomenon? Could we not also call upon God as "our Mother in heaven"? The question is not without interest, although very difficult. We do not want to involve ourselves here in the minute details of the subject to the extent we should like.[51] What we can say is that the Christian faith involved in praying to God as Father is not to be defined in sexual terms. Actually, it should express the conviction that what underlies all reality is a Principle that need appeal to no other principle, an original source of everything, which itself has no source. We would go on to say that this Principle is not some bottomless pit, lost in a void, but that it is replete with love and communion. This Father has a Son, together with whom he has originated the Holy Spirit.

When the church fathers wrote their commentaries on the Lord's Prayer, they saw in its first line the presence of the Trinity. Basically, this was because it is the Spirit of the Son, Jesus, who causes us to cry out: Abba, Father! Furthermore, to say "Father" automatically invokes the reality of the Son. As St. Cyprian said in his commentary on the Lord's Prayer: "We say Father because we have been made sons," in the Son Jesus.[52] Tertullian further enlarges the circle to include Mother Church: "We also invoke the Son in the Father because the Father and I, he says, are one (John 10:30). But we must also not forget the church, our mother. To speak the name of the Father and the name of the Son is to proclaim the mother, without whom there would be neither Father nor Son."[53]

Thus when we say "Father," we confess the ultimate mystery that penetrates and sustains the universe of beings, a mystery of love and communion. This same reality expressed by a paternal symbol could also be expressed by a maternal symbol. The Old Testament even shows traces of a maternal aspect of God: "As a mother comforts her son, so will I myself comfort you" (Isa. 66:13; see also 49:15). Pope John Paul I said that God is Father and moreover Mother. This is not the place to go into the implications of this feminine terminology. Our culture, to the extent that it is being depatriarchalized, is also being set free from a masculinizing symbolism, opening the way to approaches to God by way of the feminine. The feminine and the maternal are also worthy symbols, and quite adequately express faith in the loving mystery that generates all things. Both expressions—father and mother—point to the same ultimate reality.

How shall we pray the Lord's Prayer today? With the same spirit in which Jesus addressed the Father and with the same courage that was exhibited by the first Christian martyrs when they prayed it. In the midst of these tortures they called upon the omnipotent God who was at the same time the merciful Father.

Jesus did not live an idyllic life. His existence was a heavy commitment, weighed down with conflicts that culminated in his crucifixion. In the midst of these excruciating experiences he prayed to his beloved Father.[54] In the end he did not ask to be spared the temptations or the cup of bitterness; he sought faithfulness to his Father's will. For him also, God was both near and far at the same time. The anguishing lament from the cross reveals the painful experience of Jesus confronted with the absence of the Father. But he also felt him near: "Father, into thy hands I commit my spirit" (Luke 23:46).

In praying the Lord's Prayer, the Christian's gaze should not be directed backward in search of an ancestral past, but forward, in the direction of the advent of that kingdom promised by the Father, which is above, in heaven. The forward look and the upward look depict the attitude of hope and of faith in the love that rejoices with God the Father who is near, while also loving the Father-God who is far away. This attitude is neither alienating nor dehumanizing. It puts us in our proper place of greatness as sons and daughters in the presence of a beloved Father.

IV

Thy Name Be Hallowed

*The first Franciscans arrived in Mexico in 1524. In the inner
courtyard of the St. Francis Friary they took it upon themselves to
enlighten some high-ranking Aztec officials. The friars condemned the ancient religious beliefs. Then an Aztec scholar
stepped forward and, "with courtesy and urbanity," expressed his
displeasure at seeing the ancient customs, so esteemed by his
ancestors, attacked in this way. He said to the Christian mission-
aries:*

You have said that we do not know the Lord
who is near at hand,
the one from whom come the heavens and the earth.

You say that our gods are not the true ones.

This is what we say to you,
because we are disturbed,
because we are made uncomfortable.

Our ancestors,
who used to live upon the earth,
were not accustomed to speak in this way.

They gave us rules for our life,
they believed that these were the true rules,

41

they offered worship,
they honored the gods.

We know who it is
to whom we owe our lives,
to whom we owe our birth,
to whom we owe our conception,
to whom we owe our upbringing,
how we are to invoke the gods,
how we are to pray.

Hear this, O lords, do nothing to our people
that will bring them harm,
that will destroy them. . . .

Consider quietly and considerately, O lords,
what is really necessary.

We can have no tranquility with this way,
and certainly we do not believe this way,
we do not regard these teachings as true,
even if it means offending you.

This is what we reply to your message, O lords!

> *—From "Diálogos con los sabios indígenas,"*
> *in M.L. Portilla,* El reverso de la conquista
> *(Mexico City, 1970), pp. 23–28.*

If we are to understand well this supplication of the Lord's Prayer—thy name be hallowed—we need to recover the experience that underlies it. It is the experience already described in our reflections; we merely take it up here in greater detail.

CRY OF SUPPLICATION

The supplication finds its origin in a discovery and a desire. In this world, God the Father is neither objectively nor subjectively "hallowed" (sanctified) and glorified.[55] Circumstances objectively deny the honoring of God because of their profound internal distortions that disrupt comradely relations among persons and groups. Subjectively, men and women blaspheme the holy name of God by what they say and what they do.

First comes a cruel discovery: as has been pointed out, human society has been corrupted both in its structure and its functioning. There seems to be no corner of the world where sanity and symmetry can be found. Human conflicts and tensions do not foster growth toward justice for the great majority of humankind. Most persons have shown themselves antagonistic and destructive. They all live in a captivity that aggravates the anxiety to be free, for which they are always searching and are almost always frustrated. Objectively, we live in a situation of structural and institutionalized decadence.

Ours is more than an analytical discovery; there is also an ethical judgment. We confront the murky presence of evil, of offensiveness to God. This propagates sin, by which is meant a rupture of human beings and their sense of the transcendent, as well as a laceration of the social fabric. We can no longer look upon another's face and see a brother or sister.

Why has history come to this? The religious response, one of denunciation and accusation, may be stated thus: because the actors of history have refused to define themselves in terms of the Absolute; because the memory of God has slowly been lost; because idols of every sort have been fashioned to replace him; because the name of God is cursed. There are not a few persons who find in the misery of the world the grounds for cursing God, as did the biblical Job. Others will not tolerate God's silence in the face of injustices to the world's lowly. They intentionally reject him with the words: an impotent God cannot help us! How shall we sanctify his name?[56]

The discovery of this basic shortcoming gives rise to a desire that bursts forth in the form of a supplication: thy name be hallowed! This is the cry of Jesus' followers, addressed both to God and to their fellows. May God finally manifest his glory! May God the Father intervene, eschatologically, and put an end to what violates the divine order! May people live in such a way as to honor his name, and may they have the courage to transform the world until it is worthy of being his kingdom!

This is the experience underlying the supplication "thy name be hallowed," the experience that calls forth a cry of entreaty. To understand its content better, we shall need to clarify the two key terms: hallow (sanctify) and name.

THE SIGNIFICANCE OF "HALLOWED" AND "NAME"

Biblically speaking, "hallow" or "sanctify" is a synonym of "praise, bless, glorify"; it means to "make holy."[57] Some synonyms of "holy" are "just (righteous), perfect, good, pure." All of this is true, but it does not capture the original meaning of "holy." Holiness constitutes the axial category between religion and the Scriptures and has two interrelated dimensions. The first of these defines "being" and the second "acting"; one relates to an ontological inquiry (What is God like? What is his nature?) and the other to an ethical inquiry (How does God act? What deeds does he perform?).

The word "holy" when applied to God expresses the peculiar mode of his being. Thus, to speak of a holy God is to speak of the totally Other, the Other Dimension. God is not an extension of our world; he is a completely other reality. He is understood as apart from our being and our acting. The Scriptures say on a number of occasions that his name—that is, his nature—is holy (Isa. 6:3; Ps. 99:3, 5, 9; Lev. 11:44, 19:2, 21:8; Prov. 9:10, 30:3; 1 Chron. 16:10). He dwells, quite simply, in light inaccessible (Exod. 15:11; 1 Sam. 2:2; 1 Tim. 6:16). This means that God totally eludes us; the term "holy" thus is a negative definition of God: he is the One who is on the other side, separate (which is the etymological meaning of *sanctus:* cut off, separate, apart).

The Lord's Prayer expresses this idea when it says: Our Father in heaven. Heaven, as we have noted, is a concrete expression of what is inaccessible to man, of the infinite. Saint John says: "Holy Father" (17:11). He is near (Father) and he is remote (holy) at the same time.

This peculiar mode of being of God, as someone completely differing from us, inhibits any sort of idolatry, because idolatry means worshipping some portion of the world as God. It also condemns any manipulation of God, on the part of religious powers or of political powers. The only attitude one can have in the presence of the Holy One is that of respect, veneration, and reverence; we are in the presence of the Ineffable, of a Word without synonyms, of a Light that casts no shadow, of a Profundity that has no measured depth.

Because of this diverse nature of God, the human reaction to the Holy One is twofold, a reaction that has been analyzed in detail by religious phenomenology scholars: flight and attraction.[58] A person is terrified before the Holy One because what is encountered is unknown and without dimensions; one wants to run and hide. This was Moses' experience with the burning bush. We hear God say: "Come no nearer . . . the place where you are walking is holy ground" (Exod. 3:5). "Moses covered his face, for he was afraid to gaze on God" (Exod. 3:6). But, at the same time, the Holy One fascinates and attracts; he is charged with meaning and full of light. Moses says to himself in front of the burning bush: "I must go across to see this wonderful sight" (Exod. 3:3).

This is the ontological meaning of holy. There is also an ethical meaning. It is derived from the ontological, because acting (ethics) is the result of being (ontology). This holy God, who is so distant, so "other," and so far beyond everything that we may think or imagine, is not an aseptic or neutral God. He has ears and he can say: "I have indeed seen the misery of my people . . . I have heard their outcry against their slave-masters. I have taken heed of their sufferings" (Exod. 3:7). He takes sides; he favors the weak and opposes the oppressors; he makes a firm decision: "I have resolved to bring you up out of your misery, into . . . a land flowing with milk and honey" (Exod. 3:17). The biblical God is the Father of our Lord Jesus Christ, and he is an ethical God: he loves justice and hates iniquity. Isaiah has well said of him: "By righteousness the holy God shows himself holy" (5:16). He is absolutely just, perfect, and good; only he is radically good (Matt. 19:17), pure, without spot or blemish, and unambiguous.

God, who is ontologically remote (holy), becomes ethically near (holy): he rescues the defenseless, avenges the oppressed, identifies with the poor. God himself bridges over the gulf interposed between his holy reality and our profane reality. He rises up from his inaccessible light and crosses over into our darkness. The incarnation of the eternal Son historicizes this tender sympathy of God with his creatures.

God has overcome the distance that (ontologically) separates him from human beings, and he wants them also to overcome this distance. He wants them to be holy, as he is holy (Luke 11:13, 20:22). "There must be no limit to your goodness, as your heavenly Father's goodness knows no bounds" (Matt. 5:48; see Luke 6:36). This affirmation brings with it a requirement that is of major anthropological significance: humankind's ultimate destiny is God. Only God is the concrete expression of utopia; in other words, human beings cannot be fully or rightly understood except on the horizon of utopia. They live in the world and with the world, but the world is not enough for them; they are historical beings, but their essential dynamism calls for a break with history and their realization in metahistory.

This understanding leaves far behind it any historical totalitarianisms, especially Marxism, which understands the human person as a factor in history, reducible to a complexus of social relationships.[59] The call to be perfect and holy as the Father is perfect and holy presupposes our irreducibility with reference to our infrastructure and our ability to extrapolate beyond the boundaries of historical positivism. In a word, our calling is to heaven, not to earth; it is to God, not to an earthly paradise. This does not mean that we are summoned to retire from historical tasks; on the contrary, we must elevate the earth and history, so that together they reach their supreme ideal in God.

Summing up the meaning of this call to be holy as God is holy, we may say: human beings are called to participate in God ontically (in terms of his nature) and to imitate God ethically (in terms of action). Human beings find their true humanity in a total extrapolation of themselves, and penetration into the dimension of God. It is in the "other," in the totally Other, that they find their own true selves. This is the onotological meaning of being holy as God is holy.

How is this accomplished? Again: being holy in the ethical

sense, as God is holy, means being just, good, perfect, and pure, as God is. Anyone who walks this path is on the way to meet God. Anyone who is far from justice and goodness is also far from God, even if God's name is often on one's lips.

As may be seen, the term "holy" applied to God and to human beings both separates and unites, simultaneously. It separates, because holiness is an exclusive attribute of God, defining his proper being as distinguished from the being of the creature (world, persons, history); it unites because the holy Father becomes the ideal for human beings, the goal at which they arrive in achieving their full humanity. Between God and us there is not only a cleavage (in the ontological sense), but also communion. We are holy to the extent that we relate with the Holy One and maintain ties of communion with him. And the holy God wants to be sanctified in us: "I will show my glory in your midst" (Ezek. 28:22). The communion that takes place beyond these oppositions implies a mutual involvement of us in God and God in us, as is so excellently set forth in St. John's Gospel (10:27–29, 17:17–19). This is the universal law of salvation history, which reaches its peak in the incarnation.

We must now consider the meaning of "name."[60] Of the many possible meanings, within the context of the Lord's Prayer there is one that is most important: a name, in the Bible, designates a person, and defines his or her inner nature. To know someone's name is simply to know him or her.

God revealed his name to Moses—that is, he revealed his very self: the One who goes with the people and is always present (I am who I am—Exod. 3:14). With Isaiah in particular he reveals himself as holy—that is, as the One who transcends everything and at the same time commits himself to us (Isa. 6:3).

In Jesus, the definitive name of God is finally revealed: "O Righteous Father . . . I made thy name known to them" (John 17:25–26). Elsewhere he also speaks of God as "holy Father" (John 17:11). "Father" is the name of God. As the holy Father, God breaks through the confines of creation and yet dwells in the heavens; as the just Father, God has compassion on our lowliness and pitches his tent among us. In the language of Jesus: God is Abba, the kind, merciful Father.

LIBERATIVE SANCTIFICATION

Having pondered the meaning of the words "holy" and "name," we may now proceed to a better understanding of the supplication "thy name be hallowed (sanctified)." It means: may God be respected, venerated, and honored as he himself is, as the One who is holy, the impenetrable Mystery, fascinating and terrifying at the same time, as the One who is Yahweh (I-am-who-I-am), going with us and helping us, as the One who is Abba, a kind Father, both near and remote, totally beyond manipulation by human interests.

The least that we can do in God's presence is to recognize his otherness. He is not a human being, he does not move within the horizon of our thinking, feeling, and acting. He is the Other, and as such he is our origin and our future. If we do not recognize what he really is—someone different from ourselves—then we reduce him to a satellite of our own ego, an extension of our own desires, and this is a profound offense to him. It implies that we reject him, that we deprive him of the right to be himself (and concretely, every existent being is different), thus reducing him to a familiar, preconceived cliché.

We do not sanctify the name of God when we regard him as a "stopgap" for human weaknesses; in other words, if we call upon him and remember him only when we need help, when our infantile desires collapse around us. We then venerate God only as our own ego and put him at the service of our own interests. God is not recognized as the Other who has inestimable worth in himself, rather than by virtue of how he can help us. As long as we remain locked into a conception of God-who-helps and of religion as something good for human balance, we cannot break out of that vicious circle of our own egotism and meet with God. God is then found and venerated by us only in the extrapolation of our own vanity, in the fulfillment of desire, which, as Freud has shown, bears traits of childhood. We offend God not by denying him but by an egocentric supplication that implies that we do not recognize him as God, as someone different from ourselves and beyond the reach of our manipulations.

We do not sanctify God when our religious language (the language we use in our piety, liturgy, and theology) speaks of him as though he were an entity of this sublunar world: completely known, exhaustively defined, his will completely understood, as though we had had a personal interview with him. This reflects an irreverent attitude with a mere aura of religion; it leaves no margin for Mystery, for the Unknown, the Ineffable. It is one way of failing to sanctify God, a theological study and an understanding of the faith that domesticates revelation in the form of airtight dogmas, restricts the love of God to rules, limits the action of the Spirit to the church, and limits our encounter with the Father to outwardly recognizable religious practices.

We are not sanctifying the name of God when we erect church buildings, when we elaborate mystical treatises, or when we guarantee his official presence in society by means of religious symbols. His holy name is sanctified only to the extent that these expressions are related to a pure heart, a thirst for justice, and a reaching out for perfection. It is in these realities that God dwells; these are his true temple, where there are no idols. Origen said well, in commenting on this supplication of the Lord's Prayer: "They who do not strive to harmonize their conception of God with that which is just take the name of the Lord God in vain."[61] Thus ethics constitutes the most reliable criterion for discerning whether the God we claim to sanctify is true or false.

We sanctify the name of God when by our own life, by our own actions of solidarity, we help to build more pacific and more just human relationships, cutting off access to violence and one person's exploitation of another. God is always offended when violence is done to a human being, made in his image and likeness. And God is always sanctified when human dignity is restored to the dispossessed and the victims of violence.

Here we see emerging the challenge of a liberating sanctification in the effort to establish a world that objectively honors and venerates God by the high quality of life that it manages to create. For centuries, Christians did not consider this a central concern. Holiness was concentrated on the individual person, on complete mastery of one's passions, on purity of heart, on elevation of the spirit, on charity to one's neighbor, and on reverent submission to the ecclesiastical system with its hierarchies, canons, and time-honored paths to perfection. All of these have an inestimable and irreplaceable value; they constitute part of the ongoing task of personal sanctity and the creation of a new heart, in line with the "mind which was in Christ Jesus."[62]

But this preoccupation does not exhaust the challenge addressed to Christians; reality is more than a personal matter. It is also social. And the social aspect cannot be understood individualistically; it must be understood socially, as a woven fabric of relationships, powers, functions, interests that are sometimes antagonistic, asymmetrical, and unjust, and sometimes symmetrical, participatory, and comradely. It is in the social dimension that God the Father is most offended at present. It is important that his holy name be sanctified in this area.

God is sanctified in the arena of history by someone who is ready to do battle alongside the oppressed in the quest for their freedom from bondage. The most holy name of the Father is sanctified by someone who seeks solidarity with subordinated classes, who enters into the social process with all its conflicts and helps to construct more egalitarian relationships within the social fabric. There is another asceticism besides that of the body. It is the asceticism of bearing with defamation, persecution, imprisonment, torture, and the degradation of hard labor. Above the ascetic tower the figures of the prophet and of the political activist who confront abusive power, who raise their voices in the name of conscience and the holiness of God and cry out: "It is not lawful for you!" (Mark 6:18). "You must not victimize one another" (Lev. 25:17). Today there are all too few Christians, especially in established church communities, who are experimenting with this new sanctification of the world.

Jesus was one who walked this path. He did not proclaim the kingdom just for life's emergencies, or just for the heart, but for the four corners of the earth and for all peoples. He envisioned not only a renewed humankind but also a new heaven and a new earth. It was no accident that the New Testament presents him as the Holy One of God (Luke 4:34; Mark 1:24; John 6:69). In other words, he is the one who purifies the world and puts it in the proper state to glorify God. He once more aligns the universe of things, persons, and history to the Holy One, so that they also become holy.[63]

When the world and humankind are sanctified, the glory of

God bursts forth. In the Bible the words "glory" and "name" frequently occur in the same context: the name of God must be glorified (Ps. 86:9, 12; John 12:28). In other words, we must recognize that God is God; we must surrender to the holy Father as the Lord of history, whatever its contradictions! It is important that the world have an awareness of the true divine reality, that men and women have a religious discourse that evokes and communicates the real God, as the absolute Origin, Meaning, and Future of all things.

Sanctifying the name of the Father is the primordial task of the community of Jesus' followers—the church. The church celebrates his presence, his greatness, his victory! The church is thus itself the sacrament of the Father and of his glory in the world. To sanctify means to praise, to magnify, to glorify God despite whatever might seem to militate against it. In spite of everything, in spite of all the numerous tragedies and barbarities, history contains a sufficient manifestation of God to permit us to identify him and accept him. Tears cannot dissolve the smile, and bitterness cannot sour the joy of the heart. Here is the essential task of the Christian community: to speak of this, to reaffirm it, to celebrate it.

The supplication "thy name be hallowed" also contains an eschatological component. We discover in history that we can go beyond its possibilities and build a holy, perfect, righteous, pure world. What everyone most desires is justice, peace, and love, but they seem never to find permanent lodging in our world. Justice as a symmetry of *persons* (rather than just of social functions and social roles) is always off center. Peace as a balance between desire and its satisfaction, the absence of destructive antagonisms, and the enjoyment of freedom is always menaced. Love as self-donation to others and communion with them too easily succumbs to the mechanisms of habit, to the fetishism of rites, and the imposition of rules. We therefore supplicate God to do what history cannot: to sanctify all persons and all societies. God himself must sanctify his own name; we call upon him to manifest himself and to reveal his liberating omnipotence and dazzling glory. "It is not for your sake, you Israelites, that I am acting, but for the sake of my holy name, which you have profaned among the peoples where you have gone. I will hallow my great name, which has been profaned among the nations" (Ezek. 36:22-23). This event will signify the eschatological conclusion of history. God will be God and we shall be his sons and daughters. Everyone will sing and glorify him and magnify him: How great is the holy God in our midst! (see Isa. 12:5-6). Then we will no longer say "thy name be hallowed" as a prayer for an unfulfilled hope—for his name will then always be holy.

V

Thy Kingdom Come

Experience has taught us that it is not necessary to say "Lord, Lord" in order to do good and to enter the kingdom. In our work in the factories and in the slums, we have found examples of persons who are totally disinterested and dedicated to others, and who do not say "Lord, Lord." These persons are prepared to sacrifice their jobs, their family, and even themselves for the good of all. The gospel is present in them, and the Spirit finds realization.

We have learned to judge these persons by what they are and do, and not by the institution to which they belong or by the doctrine they profess. We invite everyone to do the same, if they wish to understand what the prophet Amos meant when he denied the special election of Israel by Yahweh and taught the practice of justice as the only source of salvation.

It is thus that we understand our struggle and our faith. We believe that we are building up the kingdom. The "we" includes those of the worker ministry and all those who struggle with us. We do not separate things from persons. We do not feel that we are better. We work with all on a basis of equality.

All those who struggle for the building of the kingdom will live in it. There will be no privileges. Righteousness is based on works; those who pass judgment on the basis of dogmas condemn themselves. There will be no room for those who reject their equals in the name of a doctrine or those who think they are saved by what they have inherited.

*They build houses and live in them, they plant and eat the fruit
of their labor.*

—*Letter of the worker ministry,
Santa Margarida basic ecclesial community, São Paulo,
published in* SEDOC *11 (1978): 362–63*

With the supplication "thy kingdom come" we get into the very
heart of the Lord's Prayer. At the same time, we are confronted
with the ultimate intention of Jesus, because the proclamation of
the kingdom of God constitutes the core of his message and the
primary motive of his activities. In order to fully comprehend the
meaning of this supplication—which burrows into the most profound depths of our anxiety and our hopes—we must begin at a
distance and dig deeply. Only then will its radicality and novelty
be appreciated.

THE NOBLEST AND DEEPEST PART
OF HUMAN NATURE

What distinguishes human beings from animals is not so much
intelligence as imagination.[64] The life of an animal is confined to
its immediate habitat; it simply mirrors the world around it. Only
the human being interprets reality, adding something to it, sym-
bolizing and fantasizing the facts of history and the world. Human beings are driven by desires that are not abated by any one
concrete activity. They have a permanent openness, whether relating to the world, to others, or to themselves. They meet their
match only when they turn to God as the Absolute, the Love, and
the Meaning that fills every desire.

The human person is not so much a *being* as a *becoming*. This
self-renewing potentiality means that any goal reached becomes a
new beginning or, better, is then seen as only one element in a
wider perspective. Present reality is merely an anticipation of
something else to come. Only human beings dream in their sleeping and waking hours of new worlds where interpersonal relationships will be always more egalitarian—a new heaven and a new
earth. Only the human person creates utopias. These utopias are

not mere escape mechanisms by which the contradictions of the present are avoided. They are part of human life, because human beings continually project, plan the future, live on promises, and feed on hope. These are the utopias that keep the absurd from taking charge of history; they disarm built-in security systems and open up the present to a promising future.

Anthropologists say that we are inhabited by a "hope principle."[65] It takes the form of a tension, of an unending search for the new, of a world without frontiers, of a questioning of the de facto circumstances, of expectation, of tomorrow, of dreams of a better life, of a world where there is no pain or sorrow or weeping or death—because all this will have passed away (Rev. 21:4)—and of hopes for a new humanity. In this hope principle we find the deepest and most radical part of human nature, the part that never dies. It is only what *is* that dies; that which *is not yet* cannot die. Hope is for what has not yet been, but is present in desire and is anticipated by the longings of the heart.

All human cultures, from the most primitive to the most advanced, have their utopias. They constitute the womb of all hope. We know those of the Judeo-Christian tradition; they speak of the transfiguration of the present world in all its relationships. We read about the reconciliation of nature, when "the wolf shall live with the sheep . . . the lion shall eat straw like cattle, the infant shall play over the hole of the cobra, and . . . they shall not hurt or destroy in all my holy mountain" (Isa. 11:6–9). God will create a new heart and a new earth; "no longer need they teach one another to know the Lord; all of them, high and low alike, shall know me [God]" (Jer. 31:34); then "they shall never again feel hunger or thirst" and nature will no longer be malevolent (Rev. 7:16). The Messianic times are represented as days when all of these utopias finally come true. "When that day comes you will ask nothing of me" (John 16:23), because God will give an answer to all the endless inquiries of the heart.

These hopes become more fervent in direct proportion to the cruelty of this world's contradictions: "In their wickedness they are stifling the truth" (Rom. 1:18), "they have bartered away the true God for a false one. . . . They are filled with every kind of mischief, rapacity, and malice; they are one mass of envy, murder, rivalry, treachery, and malevolence . . . insolent, arrogant, and boastful" (Rom. 1:25, 29–30). The lowly are exploited, the weak brutalized, the honest ridiculed, and the historical structures of injustice and sin oppress everyone.

Objectively, this situation is in defiance of God's authority. Is he not the Lord of creation? How can there be so many dimensions that elude his power and are not subject to his order? Prophets have always appeared, not allowing hope to die: one day God is going to intervene and restore everything to its original goodness and raise everything to a fullness never dreamed of in the past. The Old Testament points to it again and again: "The Lord shall reign forever and ever!" (Exod. 15:18); "I am Yahweh, he who will be here" (Exod. 3:14); "And you shall know that I am Yahweh" (Isa. 49:23; Jer. 16:21; and 54 times in Ezekiel). These are promises that nurture hope while not fundamentally changing a situation of conflict. But the overall meaning is clear: God is not indifferent to the cry that rises to heaven. He is here and will make his reign manifest!

At one point in the Old Testament era it was thought that the lordship of God would become manifest in the lordship of the king of Israel (2 Sam. 7:12–16). The king would bring justice to the poor, restore the rights of widows, and defend the orphan, thus liberating the world from its unjust principles. But within a short time the corruption of power became evident in the very kings who were supposed to represent God with the title of "Son of God" (Ps. 2:7; 2 Sam. 7:14), until the ten tribes would ask the question: "What share have we in David?" (1 Kings 12:16). The kings were corrupted, and took with them an entire people.

At another stage of Old Testament history it was thought that God would reconcile the world by means of a regulated temple worship, with its priestly orders, sacrifices, and prescriptions for holiness. God would reign from the temple, where his people would encounter him as though face to face (see Ezek. 40–43). But the prophets denounced any illusions of a worship that excluded conversion, fellowship, and mercy (Amos 5:21–24). The worship that God wants is justice and liberation of the oppressed (Isa. 1:17). The living God, more than being a God of worship, is an ethical God who despises iniquity and rejoices with the just.

Another group with a wide following in Jesus' time put its hope in a universal reconciliation in the apocalyptic sense. "Apocalyptic" (Daniel and the Revelation of St. John are the two apocalyptic books in the Scriptures) refers to a doctrine of revelation. The apocalyptics sought a secret wisdom, one that was accessible only to the initiated, by which they interpreted the signs of the times that anticipated a cosmic revolution, with the emergence of a new heaven and a new earth. This event would come suddenly and would invert every relationship: the unhappy would become happy and the happy unhappy, the poor would become rich and the rich poor, outcasts would be honored and the honored would be despised. Along with this sudden transformation would come the end of this world and the inauguration of a new heaven and a new earth.

Whereas the apocalyptics expected the kingdom to come of its own accord, the Zealots, another group of enthusiasts, felt that they should accelerate it by the use of violence. Others, such as the deeply pious Pharisees, thought that by strict observance of the divine law they would accelerate the coming of this universal transformation. They observed everything with a neurotic obsession, to the point of oppressing the weak, seeking to be absolutely faithful and thus to create the conditions for making the promises come true.

But all this was in vain. The supplication that rose to God was: Thy kingdom come! May the fullness of time come! With full confidence the prophets proclaimed: The day of the Lord comes! (Joel 3:11–15; Isa. 63:4; Mal. 4:1–5).

"HAPPY THE EYES THAT SEE WHAT YOU ARE SEEING!" (LUKE 10:23)

It is against this background of hope and anxiety that we hear the voice of Jesus of Nazareth: "The time has come; the kingdom of God is upon you; repent, and believe this good news" (Mark 1:15). This is no mere promise, as that of all the prophets before him: the kingdom *will* come! Instead, he says: the kingdom is already at hand.[66]

The unmistakable signs that the kingdom is already in effect are that "the blind recover their sight, the lame walk, lepers are made clean, the deaf hear, the dead are raised to life, and the poor are hearing the good news" (Luke 7:22). Jesus accomplished all this and then sent word of it to John the Baptist (Luke 7:18-23). The prophet Isaiah predicted these signs (Isa. 61:1-2). Jesus comments upon them preemptorily: "Today in your very hearing this text has come true" (Luke 4:21).

The kingdom of God: this is the message of hope and joy proclaimed by Jesus. The word was not frequently used in the Old Testament (see Ps. 22:28, 45:7, 103:19, 145:11; 1 Chron. 29:11; Dan. 2:44, 4:34, 5:26) and yet it constitutes (as *malkuta* in Aramaic) the verbal matrix of Jesus' message. "Kingdom" does not refer here to a territory but to the divine power and authority that now is in this world, transforming the old into new, the unjust into just, and sickness into health.

Jesus now provides the elements for a definition of the content of the kingdom.[67] He uses parables that leave no doubt as to his meaning. The kingdom is something understood to a certain extent and yet at the same time hidden and desirable. It is like a treasure hidden in a field; whoever comes upon it sells everything in order to buy the field (Matt. 13:44). It is like a precious pearl whose acquisition involves sacrificing everything (Matt. 13:45). It is like a tiny seed that grows and becomes so large that birds build their nests in it (Matt. 13:31; Mark 4:26-32). It is a force that transforms everything (Matt. 13:33).

The figure of speech used most often is that of the house or city of God, where persons sit down to eat and drink (Luke 22:30; Matt. 8:11). The Lord invites guests to his table (Matt. 22:1-14). Some enter and others are ejected (Matt. 5:20, 7:21, 18:3, 19:17, 23, 25:21, 23). There are keys for entering (Matt. 16:19). Those who live there are "born to the kingdom" (Matt. 8:12). There are many dwelling places there (John 14:2). All are invited to this house and this table, even the servants, the crippled, and those who live on the margin of society (Matt. 22:1-10). They come from the East and the West and sit down at table (Matt. 8:11). The just shine as brightly as the sun in the kingdom of their Father (Matt. 13:43). From this and other imagery one may gather that we are confronted by an absolute, fulfilled meaning, and that creation and humankind have arrived at this point.

There are three main characteristics of the kingdom announced by Jesus that have to be kept in mind. First of all, it is universal. It embraces everything; it brings liberation to such infrastructural dimensions as sickness, poverty, and death. It restructures inter-personal relationships characterized by the absence of hatred and a plenitude of fellowship. There is a new relationship with God, who is the Father of all his beloved children. The kingdom of God cannot be reduced to any dimension of this world, not even a religious dimension; Jesus regards as diabolical any temptation to reduce the kingdom to some particular segment of reality, whether political, religious, or miraculous (Matt. 4:1–11).

Secondly, the kingdom is structural: it not only embraces every-thing but it also signifies a total revolution of structure. It does not merely modify the outlines of reality but goes to the roots and brings total freedom.

Thirdly, it is definitive. Because it is of a universal and struc-tural nature, it implies the end of the world. The kingdom defines God's ultimate and final will. This world in which we live and suffer is coming to an end; there will be a new heaven and a new earth where justice, peace, and concord among all God's sons and daughters will finally triumph in the Father's great house. We can understand Jesus' exclamation: "Happy the eyes that see what you are seeing!" (Luke 10:23).

The oldest of human hopes are beginning to be realized. Utopia ceases to be fantasy and future; it becomes radiant, concrete his-tory. The kingdom is already in our midst (Luke 17:20–21) and is leavening all of reality in the direction of its fullness: "The escha-tological (final, terminal) hour of God, the victory of God, the consummation of the world is near. Indeed it is very near."[68] The kingdom must be understood as a *process*: it is already emerging, it is becoming present in the very person of Jesus, in his words, in his liberating practices, and at the same time it is open to a tomor-row when its absolute fullness will finally arrive. One needs to be prepared. You do not enter it automatically. You have to repent. This is how we understand the requirements of conversion as stated by Jesus.

The kingdom of God is constructed in opposition to the kingdom of Satan and to the presently existing diabolical struc-tures. Thus conflict is inevitable; a crisis cannot be avoided. We are urged to make a decision. The prime target is the poor. In them the new order becomes concrete, not because of their state of morality but merely because they are who they are—that is, the poor, victims of hunger, injustice, and oppression. Jesus with his kingdom wants to put an end to their degrading situation. The kingdom comes through the poor and in opposition to poverty, which will have no place in it.[69]

It is in this context that we are to understand the supplication "thy kingdom come." It complements the previous supplication: "thy name be hallowed." When God has brought into subjection all of the rebellious dimensions of creation, when he has brought everything to its happy conclusion, then the kingdom will be complete and his name will be blessed through the ages. All this is still in progress. The kingdom is a joyful state, celebrated in the present, but at the same time it is a promise that is to be realized in the future. It is a gift and a task. It is the goal of hope. Origen said it well: "The kingdom is in our midst. It is clear that when we pray 'thy kingdom come' we are praying that the kingdom of God is growing, that it is bearing fruit, and that it will reach full maturity."[70]

THE KINGDOM CONTINUES TO COME

The kingdom came in its fullest in the life and resurrection of Jesus. In him appeared the new humankind, holy relationships between persons and with the world, and a revelation of the destiny of matter, transfigured in his resurrected body. But the world still continues with its contradictions and violence. The devil still rules; he was able to eliminate Jesus and he continues to crucify the multitudes committed to building the kingdom of peace, fellowship, and justice. It is Jesus who has reminded us of the fact that the bearer of the absolute meaning of creation has been rejected.

God revealed the final end of his work: the goal is to be his kingdom. Here is an ultimate, transhistorical goal that God is achieving despite human rejections. It is like the seed of the parable: "A man . . . goes to bed at night and gets up in the morning, and the seed sprouts and grows—how, he does not know" (Mark 4:26-27). Even rejection, the cross, and sin are not insuperable obstacles to God. Even the enemies of the kingdom are at the service of the kingdom, just as those who killed Jesus were at the service of human redemption, engineered by God.

The rejection of Jesus Christ by those whose hearts are hardened demonstrates that there are "historical possibles." There are many roads that lead to the final goal, even though they contradict each other. History is not directed by fate, by a single type of behavior or a single type of development. It was Marx in his old age (1881) who recognized that one cannot make a theory concerning the laws of history, a theory of necessities, without first having a theory of the possibles that constitute the fields of practical possibilities for a given era of history—fields that do not admit of a single meaning but have a range of meanings and realizations.[71] Thus there is always a diversity of alternatives.

The cross of Christ is a demonstration of how persons, both individually and in groups, may be frustrated as they confront the ultimate meaning of creation. But God is powerful enough and merciful enough to transform this frustration into a possible path of realization. Creation in its totality is not derailed, because God will finally conquer and reign.

There is thus a guaranteed transhistorical end of things, and it is called the eschatological kingdom of God. But coexisting with this are the intrahistorical absurdities, the historical possibles that allow for denial, and the great rejection. But they will be unable to frustrate a happy outcome.

To believe in the kingdom of God is to believe in a final and happy meaning for history. It is to affirm that utopia is more real than the weight of facts. It is to locate the truth concerning the world and human beings not in the past or completely in the present, but in the future, when it will be revealed in its fullness. To pray "Thy kingdom come" is to activate the most radical hopes of the heart, so that it will not succumb to the continual brutality of present absurdities that occur at the personal and social level.

How will the kingdom of God come? For the Christian faith there is an infallible criterion that signals the arrival of the kingdom: when the poor are evangelized—that is, when justice begins to reach the poor, the dispossessed, and the oppressed. Whenever bonds of fellowship, of harmony, of participation, and of respect for the inviolable dignity of every person are created, then the kingdom of God has begun to dawn. Whenever social structures have been imposed on society that hinder persons from exploiting others, that do away with the relationships of master and slave, that favor fair dealing, then the kingdom of God is beginning to burst forth like the dawn.

St. Augustine, in commenting on the Lord's Prayer, says with great wisdom: "Thus it is the grace of living the right way that you ask for when you pray: thy kingdom come!"[72] When persons live as they should in the world, the kingdom of God is anticipated, hastened, and made concrete within history. "Living the right way" calls for many renunciations, the commitment of one's own life, and even martyrdom. "The souls of the martyrs under the altar invoke God with loud cries," Tertullian tells us in his comments on this supplication of the Lord's Prayer: "How long, sovereign Lord, holy and true, must it be before thou wilt vindicate us and avenge our blood on the inhabitants of the earth?" (Rev. 6:10). He continues: "They will obtain justice at the end of the ages. Lord, hasten the coming of your kingdom!"[73]

We need to become worthy of this supplication, "thy kingdom come!" As we follow Jesus, we lend credibility to his unlimited hope at the same time that we make this concrete in the zigzag paths of our lives. St. Cyril of Jerusalem has given us good counsel: "They who keep themselves pure in their actions, thoughts, and words are able to pray: thy kingdom come!"[74]

The supplication "thy kingdom come" is a cry that springs from the most radical hope, a hope that we often see contradicted, but which we never give up despite everything, as we hope for the revelation of an absolute meaning that is to be realized by God in all of creation. Those who thus pray commit themselves confidently to him who has been shown to be stronger than the strong man (Mark 3:27) and who therefore has the power to convert the old into the new and to inaugurate a new heaven and a new earth, where the reconciliation of everyone with everyone and everything will be the rule of the day. We can already give thanks for this promise inasmuch as the supplication "thy kingdom come" is being heard and answered: "We give thee thanks, O Lord God, sovereign over all, who art and who wast, because thou hast taken thy great power into thy hands and entered thy reign" (Rev. 11:17).

VI

Thy Will Be Done

. . . And the woman whom I had known for some years called me aside and said in a mysterious tone of voice: "Father, I am going to show you a secret. Come!"

We entered a room. In the bed was her son. He was a monster. He had an enormous head, like that of an adult. His little body was like that of a child. His eyes stared up at the ceiling. His tongue darted in and out like that of a snake.

"My God!" I exclaimed in a kind of groan.

"Father," she said, "I have looked after this child for eight years now. He knows only me. I love him very much. Almost no one knows about it."

She concluded: "God is good. God is our Father. . . ."

And she looked upward, serene: "Your will be done on earth as it is in heaven!"

This was all she said. And she said everything.

I left without saying a word. With my head bowed. The child frightened me. The mother caused me perplexity. There was only one thought in my mind: "Woman, what faith you have!" (Matt. 15:28).

In order to understand this third supplication of the Lord's Prayer—thy will be done on earth as in heaven—we have to return to the context of what we have said thus far.[75] Our gaze is

lifted heavenward and our face is kept turned toward God. Amid
the misery of this world and the negation of historical meaning,
we dare to cry: Our Father. The world does not recognize God; it
blasphemes his holy name (his reality). It is with full enthusiasm
that we pray: thy name be hallowed! The new heaven and the new
earth have already begun to appear in the coming, the message,
and the presence of Jesus. The kingdom is already in the process
of realization; but the fullness, unhappily, is still delayed. It is
with anxious expectation that we pray: thy kingdom come.

No matter how much we pray and commit ourselves to follow
the steps of Jesus, we never actually see the approach of the
kingdom. The antichrist continues his work and the devil still has
his followers. We may be visited by a feeling of desolation: Why
does God delay? What is his will, after all? And in this context we
continue to pray: thy will be done on earth as in heaven! What
does this petition mean? It is important to know the will of God,
how our own will is coordinated with God's will and what value is
to be found in historical patience.

WHAT IS THE WILL OF GOD?

This is one of the most basic questions confronting any
religious-minded person. We want to do the will of God, but what
is this will, concretely, for any given situation? Where do we find
it?

Before looking for an answer, we need to take stock of the prior
experience behind the supplication "thy will be done on earth as
in heaven." Anyone who prays this presupposes that our present
world is not doing the will of God and that humanity is rebelling
against God's will. As we have seen, our human history resists
being conformed to the will of God; justice seems to be silenced,
the rich are getting richer at the expense of the poor, more and
more reduced to a kind of "fuel" for the production processes of
economic and social elites. Only the elite have a planned life; the
great majority are not doing what they would like to do or what
they are fitted for, but what has been determined for them by their
social status.

There is a thunderously silent protest rising to heaven, provoked by all this suffering, humankind's oppression of human-

kind, the powerful on the backs of the weak. There is no fantasy capable of exorcising all the ghosts that have been turned loose in the minds of millions, worn out with their sobbing and drowned in their own tears. We have an almost insuperable difficulty accepting ourselves; the way that leads to "the other" is blocked with almost immovable obstacles. One who prays "thy will be done" must have overcome the temptation to despair that is implied in this situation.

We discover another kind of silent protest on the part of the person who refuses to do the will of God. There is a reluctance, a selfishness that insists on doing one's own will without asking whether or not it harmonizes with the will of God. It is not uncommon for the protest to be an open one, as the many despondent ones of history refuse to admit that there is a sovereign will to be found in the gloomy scenario of contradictions that history cannot conceal. To pray "thy will be done" implies the ability to get out of oneself, to believe in the power of God's love despite human ill will, and to have confidence that human malice can be overcome by divine mercy.

We have to listen to all the overtones that are present in this supplication of the Lord's Prayer. We shall not deal with all the main points of all the problems involved in doing the will of God. We wish to remain within the context of Jesus' prayer, the Lord's Prayer. What was the will of God for Jesus? The answer comes at three levels that need to be differentiated and emphasized.

For Jesus, the unmistakable will of God is to establish God's kingdom. Thus the proclamation of the kingdom constitutes the central theme of his preaching, as we have noted before. God wants to be Lord of his creation, and this happens to the extent that every disorderly element in creation is subjugated (sickness, unjust human relations, abuses of power, death—in a word, sin) and that all this is brought to its maturity. Then and only then will the kingdom have been established.

The liberation of creation and its maximum extension is God's immutable will. Jesus did not just proclaim this will of God; he transformed it into reality by the things he did. In this sense, the supplication "thy will be done" repeats and intensifies what precedes it—that is, "thy kingdom come." Luke, in his version of the Lord's Prayer, omits this supplication, possibly because it adds nothing to the preceding supplication. Furthermore, the original Greek of Matthew has: "May your will *come about* (*genetheto*)," an expression that is also applied to the kingdom.

In St. John's Gospel, Jesus says clearly: "It is meat and drink for me to do the will of him who sent me until I have finished his work" (John 4:34). In another passage he makes the statement: "My aim is not my own will, but the will of him who sent me" (John 5:30). And he clarifies this statement with another that adds an additional meaning to the word "kingdom": "It is his will that I should not lose even one of all that he has given me, but to raise them all up on the last day" (John 6:39).

To love no one and to raise each one up to fullness of life—this is what is meant by the expression "kingdom of God." St. Paul uses another terminology to express the same idea of this kingdom that God wants to establish: "He has made known to us his hidden purpose—such was his will and pleasure determined beforehand in Christ—to be put into effect when the time was ripe; namely, that the universe, all in heaven and earth, might be brought into a unity in Christ" (Eph. 1:9-10). The kingdom (or will) of God is realized when everything reaches its full unity and perfection. Its mediation is effected in Jesus Christ, who has proclaimed and brought into being the will and kingdom of God.

This kingdom is being built in opposition to the kingdom of Satan, who represents opposition to the will of God. He is the prince of this world (John 12:31, 14:30, 16:11; Eph. 2:2)—that is, he also possesses power and maintains an organization. In his public life, Jesus confronted him with his words and deeds (Luke 12:20; Mark 3:22-26). He subjected Satan to a severe defeat when he died on the cross (John 12:31-32, 14:30, 16:11; 1 Cor. 2:8). But Satan continues as the great antagonist (2 Cor. 4:4; 2 Thess. 2:7). In the end, however, he will be decisively defeated (Rev. 20:10).

To pray, in this sense, that God's will be done is to call upon God himself to bring about his kingdom. He has already officially inaugurated this kingdom in history, through Jesus. From this standpoint, the kingdom does not depend upon human activity; it is the kingdom of *God*; God will realize his eternal plan (Eph. 1:4), which is to make creation the locus of his presence, his glory, and his love. To pray "thy will be done" is to ask that this take place quickly; to ask that God not delay in accomplishing what he himself has proposed to do!

We have considered the will of God as something that belongs to God—his kingdom and his designs. But this will of God, besides its objective aspect, also has its subjective side, in that it is to be accepted and realized by human beings. The kingdom (the objective will of God) consists basically of a gift and an offering. God is always the first to love (1 John 4:19).

The kingdom and everything that comes from God is structured as a proposal, not as an imposition; it is a gesture of invitation and not a preemptive command. This is because God is love (1 John 4:8) and the law of love is that of a free commitment, an uncoerced offering, and an acceptance made in freedom. We must become open to the gift of God. The Scriptures issue a call to this human process of conversion. It is necessary for the kingdom to come to our world, to become de facto history.[76] Thus Jesus, in his very first proclamation, announces that the coming of the kingdom is already in progress, and at the same time he makes the plea: Be converted and believe this good news (Mark 1:15).

The coming of the kingdom is not automatic, with no collaboration on the part of human beings. The kingdom is of God, but it has to be appropriated by us. God does not save the world and humanity by himself. He involves the human race in this messianic project in such a way that one person becomes a sacrament of salvation for another. And this cooperation is of such a decisive nature that our eternal salvation depends upon its fulfillment. Thus we are dealing with a course of action that is demanded by the supreme Judge, particularly for what relates to providing assistance, solidarity, and liberation for the oppressed: "Anything you did for one of my brothers here, however humble, you did for me . . . anything you did not do for one of these, however humble, you did not do for me" (Matt. 25:40, 45).

It is not enough to say "Lord, Lord" and thus decipher the mystery that Jesus has hidden under the seeming frailty of an unexpectedly unspectacular messianic mission; only those are truly saved "who do the will of my heavenly Father" (Matt. 7:21). What is this "will"? We do not have to go far or dig deeply to find out: it is to live out discipleship to Jesus, to have the same mind that he had (Phil. 2:2, 5), to be oriented by the spirit of the Beatitudes and the Sermon on the Mount (Matt. 5–7). This conversion constitutes a true rebirth, and "unless a man has been born over again, he cannot see the kingdom of God" (John 3:3).

God does not desire the death of sinners, but that they be converted and live (see Ezek. 18:23, 32, 33:11; 2 Peter 3:9). The "good, acceptable and perfect will of God" is that we not become "adapted to the pattern of this present world, but with minds remade and your whole nature transformed" (Rom. 12:2). Paul summed it all up: "This is the will of God, that you be holy" (1 Thess. 4:3). And we have the guarantee that "he who does the will of God stands forever more" (1 John 2:17). We even have God's promise that he will not abandon anyone who seeks him and that we should not "live for the rest of the days on earth for the things that men desire, but for what God wills" (1 Peter 4:2). We pray that he make us "perfect in all goodness so as to do his will" (Heb. 13:21), because it is he, in the final analysis, who "is at work in you, inspiring both the will and the deed" (Phil. 2:13).

Thus, when we pray "thy will be done," we mean: your will be done *for us*; we may be faithful to the task you assign us and to the gift of your kingdom, seeking to live in accordance with the newness of the message, the attitudes, and the life of Jesus Christ. Whenever anyone does the will of God, it is not only for the person but also for the world that the kingdom of God comes.[77]

The will of God further involves a component of patience, of humble abandonment to the mystery of God, and even of resignation. We know what the will of God is: the realization of the kingdom on the part of God and on the part of humanity. But this knowledge does not give us an understanding of the postponement of the new heaven and the new earth. Why does God not accomplish his will speedily? Why does he not inspire men and women to decide more quickly to live according to the standards of the kingdom? History continues in its ponderous zigzag course, with its absurdities, its unjust, sinful mechanisms, and the constant questionings that our hearts send heavenward. This experience becomes even more disturbing when we note that often the best projects, the most highly motivated intentions, and the most holy causes are defeated. It is not uncommon for the righteous to become marginal to society, for the wise to be ridiculed, and for saints to be executed. We see the frivolous triumph, we see the biased and dishonest turn a profit, and we see mediocre persons command the destinies of entire nations.

In this context, praying "thy will be done" means abandoning oneself to the mysterious designs of God. Here is a resignation that does not mean choosing the easiest path or the one that is most reasonable: true wisdom is not measured by the criteria that we use with our limited powers of reasoning, but by the parameters of God's wisdom, which is as high above us as the heavens are above the earth. If we are to accept the mysterious path of God, even when we see and understand nothing about it, then we need to renounce ourselves and our own plans. This requires detachment from our own will, even when it has been honestly and genuinely oriented. The titanism of a will that will dare anything but that is not submitted to a greater will is not an expression of the most human part of human nature. True greatness of spirit is to recognize the limits of one's range of possibilities and the finiteness of one's forces; this human condition opens up the possibility of a humble decision for a more transcendent plan that involves each of us and all of creation.

To pray "thy will be done" is equivalent to saying: let what God wants be done! There is no element of complaint or despair in this, but a confident commitment, like that of a child snuggling into the arms of its mother. God is Father and Mother of infinite goodness. He has his eternal plan; we also have our plans. As children who have never quite understood everything that our father does nor the full import of his words, so also we, as we pursue our pilgrimage, do not comprehend all the dimensions of history, nor can we understand the total meaning of what is being realized. It is without bitterness that we recognize the finite nature of our own viewpoints and commit ourselves to him who is the beginning and the end, in whose hands rests our entire itinerary.

This abandonment finds corroboration in the ancient wisdom of our Western culture, in men such as Seneca, Epictetus, Socrates, Marcus Aurelius, and others.[78] Nor is it absent in the Old Testament (see 1 Sam. 3:18; Tobit 3:6; Ps. 135:6, 143:10; Wisd. 9:13–18; 1 Macc. 3:60; 2 Macc. 1:3–4). According to the author of the Epistle to the Hebrews, Jesus, when he came into the world, said: "Sacrifice and offering thou [God] didst not desire, but thou

hast prepared a body for me. Whole-offerings and sin-offerings
thou didst not delight in. Then I said: 'Here I am: as it is written of
me in the scroll, I have come, O God, to do thy will' " (Heb.
10:5–7).

In the garden of Gethsemane, when Jesus saw that his violent
death was inevitable, he became profoundly distressed. But his
serene abandonment to the will of God prevailed: "Father, if it be
thy will, take this cup away from me. Yet not my will but thine be
done" (Luke 22:42). Here we see the profound and real humanity
of Jesus. He, like us, is also a pilgrim and wanderer; he shares the
anxieties of one who does not know everything immediately and is
not aware of every step toward the will of God.

There is no doubt that Jesus knew the will of God; but because
of his human condition he still had not been enthroned in the
fullness of God's kingdom, where everything is transparent; thus
he had to search concretely for the will of God in the here and
now. What steps should he take? How could he best realize the
known will of God? Jesus was confronted with his human limitations and with his own anxiety. He was subject to anger toward
those who did not accept his message. He accepted this situation;
he did not ask for the forces of heaven to come to his aid (see
Matt. 26:53). Here the Epistle to the Hebrews sheds some light
when it testifies to this acceptance of Jesus. We translate the passage directly from the Greek, in an attempt to capture the spirit of
the original:

> Christ, during his mortal life, directed to him who had the
> power to set him free, even from death, the insistent suppli-
> cation of his own pain and his own tears; he was heard pre-
> cisely because he accepted the pain and the tears with docil-
> ity. And so, though he was the Son, he understood from his
> own suffering that the destiny of humankind is reached only
> by acceptance *[hypakoe]*. Besides achieving this destiny to
> arrive at the fullness of his own being *[teleiotheis]*, he be-
> came the basis for eternal salvation for all those who follow
> his path. Thus God has appointed him as our High Priest
> [Heb. 5:7–9].

It is no wonder, then, that Jesus' last word, according to St.
Luke, was an exclamation of total abandonment: "Father, into

thy hands I commit my spirit!" (Luke 23:46). Here is the expression of radical human freedom: to commit oneself to a greater being who commands the ultimate meaning of every quest and who knows the why of every failure. The expression that is a part of our daily language—"God willing"—has a profound theological root (see Rom. 1:10, 15:32; 1 Cor. 4:19, 16:7; Acts 18:21; James 4:15). It presupposes that the true center of the human person is not the "I" but the (divine) "thou." Human freedom will come to pass only if it is oriented toward this center; then the will of God is realized and the kingdom is at hand.[79]

ON EARTH AS IN HEAVEN

In the language of the Middle East and the Old Testament, the words "heaven and earth" are used to provide a spatial definition of the totality of God's creation (see Matt. 5:18, 24:35). Thus God is "Lord of heaven and earth" (Matt. 11:25) and the resurrected Christ received authority over heaven and earth (Matt. 28:18). To pray "thy will be done on earth as in heaven" means: to do the will of God everywhere and always. The kingdom of God is not and never will be a *specific geographical region* of creation; it is the *whole* of creation (heaven and earth) transfigured. The will of God encompasses the totality of his creation. For our part, our conversion, our sanctification (our own part in realizing the will of God), cannot be restricted to a particular dimension of human life, such as just to the heart or exclusively to the religious or ethical field; sanctification must occur in every sphere into which our existence extends.

Today we are especially sensitive to structural sin and social injustice; this is of essential importance in realizing holiness in social relationships, and in economic, political, and cultural mechanisms. There is no area of space that is to be closed off from the transformation intended by the kingdom of God; the leavening action of the new heaven and the new earth is to begin in everything. All of these requirements are bound up in the expression "on earth as in heaven"—in other words, doing the will of God in everything and in all dimensions.

On the other hand, the correlation, on earth *as* in heaven, allows us to enrich the above interpretation. In line with biblical thinking, God already reigns in heaven. That is where his throne is (see Isa. 66:1; Matt. 5:34–35; Ps. 103:19–21). All the inhabitants of heaven (angels and the righteous) do the will of God fully, as Psalm 103 says so explicitly. Earth is the place where the will of God is still opposed, where God exercises his historical magnanimity and patience (see Rom. 2:4). The supplication means: just as the will of God is already done in heaven, so let it also be done on earth as soon as possible. May the kingdom that is already victorious in heaven be also established on earth! Origen has an excellent comment on this petition: "If the will of God were done on earth as it is in heaven, earth would no longer be earth . . . we would then all be in heaven."[80]

Thus everything is to arrive at the point of full reconciliation: heaven is to come down to earth and earth is to be raised up to heaven. And then the end will come: God will be all and in all (1 Cor. 15:28). As long as this has not happened, then we must always and everywhere pray: thy kingdom come; thy will be done on earth as in heaven!

VII

Give Us Today
Our Daily Bread

Early in the morning, as they do every day,
the young men are contesting with the dogs
over rights to the garbage can.

They mix and remix,
they take out what is edible from the garbage.

And they share this rotten refuse with the dogs.

In a dog-eat-dog world,
where there is no pity,
this is how God is left to answer
the prayer of the hungry ones:
give us today our daily bread!

Today—no, all week—
the bread on our table has not been the same.
It was bitter bread,
full of the curses of the poor
who had been begging God for it.

It regained its taste and goodness
only when it was shared with those starving creatures,
the boys and the dogs.

This petition marks a turning point in the Lord's Prayer. The first part was directed toward heaven: the divine reality of God as Father, the transcendent one (in heaven) and at the same time nearby (our Father) who must always be sanctified, whose kingdom is to come and be made history among us, thus achieving the ultimate will of God. The tone is solemn and the phrases are cadenced. Now, in the second part, our gaze is turned toward the earth and toward humankind and its needs: the bread necessary for life, forgiveness for disruptions of fellowship, strength against temptation, and deliverance from evil. The phrases are long, and their tone conveys the affliction that is so much a part of human life. In the first part of the prayer, God's concerns are dealt with; in the second part, human concerns. Both belong in the prayer.

In the second part, we see no mysticizing or spiritualizing: here is human life in its historical, infrastructural, biological, and social concreteness, forever threatened. It is not concerned only with humanity; God is also involved. This makes of it the stuff of prayer and supplication. Thus there is no competition between the vertical concerns of God and the horizontal concerns of humanity. Both meet under the rainbow of prayer. The unmistakable union of material and spiritual, of human and divine, constitutes the force emanating from the mystery of the incarnation. In the kingdom of God there is an interlocking of material and spiritual, of human nature and cosmos, of creation and Creator. We should not be surprised, then, if in the Lord's Prayer the two are brought together; here the most sublime encounters that which is most down-to-earth. That which is routine, obvious, and ordinary —bread—has a standing both before God and before humanity. The Lord's Prayer vigorously reaffirms this truth in defiance of spiritualizers.[81]

BREAD: THE DIVINE DIMENSION OF MATTER

This petition centers on the word "bread." We need to deal with this word, pure and simple, before dealing with the qualifications that go with it ("our" and "today" or "each day"). The word "bread" has a highly significant content; we find here an important aspect of anthropology—that is, the study of the human phenomenon. The meaning of bread goes beyond its physical and chemical composition. It is a symbol of all human food, the food that we cannot do without (Prov. 20:13, 30:8; Ps. 146:7; Lev. 26:5; Eccles. 9:7; Sir. 31:23–24). Bread is the "bread of life" (John 6:35).

Human life is indissolubly connected with a material infrastructure. No matter how high the spirit soars, no matter how deep our mystical probings, or how metaphysical our abstract thinking, the human being will always be dependent on a piece of bread, a cup of water—in short, on a handful of matter. The material infrastructure is so important that ultimately we find it the root and ground of everything we think about or plan or do. It is like the foundation of a building: it makes reference, ultimately, not only to the floors of the building and the furniture found in its rooms, but also the persons who live there. It is the condition that makes possible human existence and survival. It is thus like the human food that is symbolized by bread: life depends upon it, upon its opaque materiality, upon its material substance. Life is more than bread, but at any given moment it cannot get along without bread.

In theological terms, the human infrastructure is so important that God connects being saved and being lost with a just and comradely concern that we may or may not put into practice. Thus, in the final analysis, we are to be judged by the supreme Judge according to criteria found in the infrastructure: whether or not we have looked after the hungry, the naked, the thirsty, the prisoner. Our eternal destiny is thus ultimately involved with bread, with water, with clothing, and with solidarity with others (see Matt. 25:31–46).

Thus the stomach assumes an importance in line with that of the heart and the head. There is no prayer or spiritual activity that takes the place of bread, or of the frequently heavy labor required to earn it and to put it on the table of the hungry. Nor can pious speech quell the hunger of a starving person. God wants us to earn bread with our work, which involves time, sweat, tears, and some degree of remoteness from God, because we are so busy with earthly things instead of those of heaven. God wants us to be concerned not only with his affairs, his kingdom, his will, and his name, but also with human affairs, human needs, human hunger, the desperate need for protection and salvation. Human beings are not here on earth just for God, but also for themselves. God wants it that way. To pray to God means to include everything and offer it to the Father—both God's affairs and humanity's affairs.[82]

If we observe closely, we will see that a turning has been made in the Lord's Prayer. In the first three supplications (thy name be hallowed, thy kingdom come, thy will be done) we concern ourselves with God's affairs. In the next four petitions (concerning bread, forgiveness of transgressions, temptation, and deliverance from evil) it is God who is concerned with our affairs. These two dimensions must never be separated: the Lord has brought them together in his prayer. We should never feel ashamed of our needs. God cares about hunger; it is his intention to hear our pleas and to fill the hungry mouth. This provides a guarantee of life, the most precious gift that we have received from God.

Thus matter becomes the vehicle of a divine reality: it is sacramental; it becomes evident in proportion to our assurance that bread, according to the Scriptures, constitutes the historical symbol of the kingdom of God, represented as a great feast. It is the temporal sign of the eternal food that guarantees everlasting life. Bread conveys the promise of a fullness of life; even more, it makes present, right now, in the midst of this journey of hungry pilgrims, the bread that completely satisfies humankind's salvific hunger—that is, Jesus and his kingdom.

All this is contained in that monosyllabic, everyday, natural, simple word: bread.

THE SIGNIFICANCE OF "OUR": THE SECRET OF HAPPINESS

The need for bread is an individual matter, but the satisfaction of that need cannot be an individual effort; it must be that of a community. Thus we do not pray "my Father," but "our Father." There is here a profound meaning in Jesus' prayer. It is true that the Old Testament recognizes individual satisfaction: "Eat your food and enjoy it" (Eccles. 9:7); "share your bread with the hungry" (Isa. 58:7). But with Jesus we achieve a full awareness of human fellowship.[83] We have a Father who belongs to all of us, because he is *our* Father; we are all his offspring, and thus we are all brothers and sisters. Mere personal satisfaction of hunger without considering the others would be a breach of that fellowship. A person is not just interested in deadening hunger and surviving "somehow." Eating means more than a mere satisfaction of nutritional requirements; it is a communitarian act and a communion rite. Eating is not as enjoyable or fully human if done in sight of the misery of others, the Lazaruses at the foot of the table, waiting for the leftover crumbs. Daily bread provides a basic and necessary happiness for life. If there is to be any happiness, it must be communicated and shared. That is how it is with bread: it is *human* bread to the extent that it is shared and supports a bond of communion. Then happiness is found, and human hunger is satisfied.

Beneath the bread that we consume daily is hidden a whole network of anonymous relationships of which we need to remind ourselves. Before it reaches our table it receives the labor of many hands. The seed is planted in the ground; it has to be tended as it grows. Many hands harvest the grain or maneuver the powerful machinery. Many other hands store the grain and make the bread. Then there are the thousands of distribution points. In all this we find the greatness and the wretchedness of human nature. There can be relationships involving exploitation. Tears are shed over every loaf that we so calmly eat, but we also sense the fellowship and the sharing. Daily bread encompasses the entire human universe in its lights and shadows.

This bread that is jointly produced must be distributed and consumed in concert with others. Only then can we truthfully ask for *our* daily bread. God does not hear the prayer that asks only for *my* bread. A genuine relationship with God calls for maintaining a relationship with others. When we present God with our own needs, he wants us to include those of our brothers and sisters. Otherwise the bonds of fellowship are severed and we live only for ourselves. We all share the same basic necessity; collective satisfaction of that need makes us brothers and sisters.

When the bread that we eat is the result of exploitation, it is not a bread blessed by God. It may supply the chemical needs of nutrition but fail to nourish human life, which is human only when lived within the framework of justice and fraternity. Unjust bread is not really our bread; it is stolen; it belongs to someone else. The great medieval mystic, Meister Eckhart, well said: "They who do not give to another what belongs to the other are not eating their own bread, but are eating both their bread and the other's."[84]

The thousands of hungry persons in our cities and the millions of starving persons in our world question the quality of our bread: it is bitter because it contains too many children's tears; it is hard because its substance embraces the torture of so many empty stomachs. It does not deserve to be called *our* bread. If the bread is to be ours, then we must transform the world and deliver society from the mechanisms that permit wealth to be maintained at the expense of bread taken from the mouths of others.

Bread calls us to a collective conversion. This condition must be fulfilled if our prayer is not to be vain and pharisaical. The gospel forbids me to ask only for myself, disregarding the needs of others known by me. Only *our* bread is God's bread.

EACH DAY: BREAD NECESSARY FOR TIME AND FOR ETERNITY

To the concept of "our" bread we add a very important qualifying phrase: "daily" or "each day" or "for the morrow." The Greek term used is *epiousios*.[85] The matter of its exact meaning is a problem for the experts, because this word, as Origen had already observed in his commentary on the Our Father,[86] has no parallel in any secular Greek text (except perhaps the Hawara papyrus of Upper Egypt, which dates from the fifth century A.D.)[87] and seems to have been coined by the evangelists. Thus our only recourse is philological analysis. There are three possibilities.

One interpretation derives *epiousios* from *epi* ("over, upon, through," etc.) - *einai* (from the verb "to be"). *Ousios* is an adjective; it would have the meaning: "bread for the day that is now, daily bread, the bread given day by day." The most ancient Latin translations (the *Itala*) understood it thus. One may also read it as: the bread "necessary for existence, indispensable for existence" *(epi ousia)*.

The bread that provides for our basic needs is each day's bread, as we commonly pray for it. In the Vulgate, St. Jerome translated the Matthean version of this petition *panis supersubstantialis* (which is a literal translation: *epi* = *super*, and *ousios* = *substantialis*), whereas for the Lukan version he translated it *panis quotidianus*.

The second interpretation understands *epiousios* as a derivative of *epi* + *ienai* ("to come" or "arrive"). The resultant meaning would be: "our bread for the morrow, for the day that is coming, our future bread." In his comments on the Gospel of Matthew, St. Jerome mentions that the Gospel of the Hebrews (an apocryphal Semitic writing) translates *epiousios* ("supersubstantial") with the Hebrew word *machar*, which means "tomorrow"—that is, the future.[88] The reading would then be: "give us today (or "each day") our bread for the morrow."

The third interpretation, which is the most recent, derives from the discovery that there are many compound words such as *epiousios* whose prefix has no specific meaning; it is an "empty" prefix.[89] Words of this kind are found in every language. In English, for example, we may speak of "loosening" a rope or shoestrings, or we may speak of "unloosening" them; both words are identical in meaning, even though the prefix "un" normally indicates a negation or opposite meaning to that of the root word. In French, there are words such as *partir* ("to depart") and *départ* ("departure"); *chercher* ("to investigate") and *recherche* ("investigation"). The prefix *de* of *départ* and the *re* of *recherche* add nothing to the root meanings of their respective words. In Greek there are thirteen compound adjectives formed with *ousios* (with the prefixes *an, en, omoi, hyper,* etc.), all of which have the substantive *ousia* as their root (meaning "substance" or "essence").

In the case with which we are concerned, in the combination *epi* +*ousios* the prefix *epi* is not to be translated *super*—as St. Jerome would have it—because *epi* conveys the idea of "concerning" or "belonging to." Thus *epiousios* would mean: "that which concerns the essence, the essential, the substantial." But this is already the common meaning of the word *ousios* without any prefix. At most, the prefix would have an intensive function, reinforcing the original meaning; but it adds nothing to the original meaning. There are various words in the Greek language with the prefix *epi* where it does not enrich the root (*epinephes* = "cloudy"; *epidorpios* = "relating to stew, stewed"; *epikephalios* = "relating to the head"). The word *epiousios* would seem to be of the same type. The prefix *epi* carries no special meaning. The phrase would thus mean: "essential bread, substantial bread, the bread necessary for life." But what is necessary for life belongs to our day-by-day experience, to each day. Thus the third interpretation approximates the first.

Which of these explanations is closest to the mark? Is it tomorrow's bread or is it today's? Both meanings are possible. To decide for one meaning or the other requires more than philological reasoning. Exegetes or theologians will decide upon the meaning that best corresponds to their conception of the historical Jesus and his message. Thus those who tend to interpret Jesus of Nazareth within an eschatological framework prefer the second meaning: give us today the bread of the future.[90] Others, who understand Jesus and his message from a noneschatological perspective (Jesus was not expecting an immediate end to history and the final coming of the kingdom), will interpret *epiousios* as bread for today (the bread that we need each day), the essential and substantial bread for our pilgrimage on earth (the first and third interpretations).

This problem of the Lord's Prayer is not solved just by recourse to historical criticism and its reference to the historical Jesus. The Lord's Prayer was the most important prayer of the Christian community at that time, for whom the *eschaton* was situated in an unknown future. It is in terms of the present situation, the temporal world, as history is being made day by day, that the Lord's Prayer is to be prayed today. The words take on a "church community" significance that may differ from that of its origin with the historical Jesus. In other words, to the primeval meaning that Jesus himself attached to it is added another, conferred upon it by the early community, already organized into churches, finally culminating in a meaning that we attribute to it today, in our own situation. All of these meanings can be true. The most ancient meaning need not be the only correct one; it is like a fountainhead that gives rise to other interpretations, all of which add meaning to a life of prayer.

Thus, in this intricate discussion of the original meaning of the expression *epiousios*, as to whether it means future bread, daily bread, or essential bread, we see three levels of meaning. Each of them presupposes the other and is interlocked with it. All of these interpretations are an echo of the same expression, "our bread for each day."

For my part, I feel that the meaning conveyed by the historical Jesus is that of future bread, tomorrow's bread. This choice is based on a conviction, which I cannot fully explain here, that the historical Jesus was motivated in the context of an apocalyptico-eschatological perspective.[91] He lived with the expectation that the kingdom of God was about to break forth, but without a clear-cut delineation of the "times and seasons" of its inauguration.

The hard core of his proclamation, the Sermon on the Mount, the radical nature of his demands—all lend a high probability to this interpretation. In line with such an interpretation, the gospels attest repeatedly that the kingdom of God is comparable to a feast. The true "substantial" bread will be served at the heavenly table. Our petition for food (bread) is related to this heavenly banquet. Thus we read in Luke 14:15, "Happy the man who shall sit at the feast in the kingdom of God." The same eschatological term is found in another text of Luke, 6:21: "How blessed are you who now go hungry; your hunger will be satisfied." On other occasions Jesus speaks of "eating and drinking at my table in the kingdom" (Luke 22:30), and he says that "many will come from East and West to feast with Abraham, Isaac, and Jacob in the kingdom of Heaven" (Matt. 8:11). The Apocalypse describes heaven as a place where the righteous will no longer be hungry (Rev. 7:16). This future bread in the eternal kingdom of the Father is the object of our petition, "gave us this bread now." In other words, "May your kingdom come soon! Bring about your liberating intervention, Lord, as quickly as possible. Take us to the banquet where the real substantial food (bread) is served, the food that imparts eternal life."

The Old Testament provides some basis for this eschatological interpretation. Concerning the manna, it is stated in Exodus: "I will rain down bread from heaven for you. Each day . . . a day's supply" (Exod. 16:4). In Psalm 78:24, we find: "And he rained down upon them manna for them to eat and gave them the grain of heaven." Jesus himself refers to this text when he says: "It was not Moses who gave you the bread from heaven; my Father gives you the real bread from heaven" (John 6:32).

This interpretation—of giving us today the bread of tomorrow (the future)—seems to fit well into the framework of Jesus' eschatological mentality. But note carefully: the meaning of this future, eschatological bread in the kingdom of God is rooted in the materiality of a concrete, historical bread. Any real symbol (bread of heaven) has its basis in concrete reality (bread of earth). No real symbol exists in its own right; there is always some reference to the foundation on which it is constructed. In other words, to ask for the bread of heaven (future bread) we must at the same time ask for material bread for our bodies. Otherwise we could not understand what is meant by the really substantial bread of the kingdom of God. Deprive the symbol of its reality, and it becomes nothing. Heavenly bread, deprived of earthly bread, is incomprehensible. Here we are not retracting anything that we stated above as to the down-to-earth reality of the bread that nourishes our lives, which allows us to be promised the bread that actually bestows eternal life in the kingdom of the Father.

In the noneschatological view of Jesus, the more reasonable interpretation of *epiousios* is bread for each day, "daily bread." This was the meaning arrived at by the Christian community that dwelt on the fringes of history and tried to live the ideal demanded by Jesus, of a serene abandonment to divine providence.[92] The Lord taught his disciples "not to be anxious about tomorrow" (Matt. 6:34), and not to be anxious about what to eat or what to wear (Matt. 6:25). In sending the disciples on a mission, he advised them not to take along any provisions: "no bread, no pack, no money in their belts" (Mark 6:8). The evangelical ideal consists in living a life of poverty, completely abandoned to the ministrations of divine providence. God would provide the basic necessities. It is a radical ideal. There have always been spirits, down through history, who took the words of the Lord seriously and lived this kind of life.

What is being asked for by this petition in the Lord's Prayer is the bread necessary for each day. Even the Old Testament taught: "Give me neither poverty nor wealth; provide me only with the food I need" (Prov. 30:8; see also Sir. 40:29). Thus one does not ask God for wealth or a comfortable life or for convenience; but neither does the Old Testament exalt poverty as the absence of what is necessary. It asks only for what is sufficient to keep the petitioner alive for today. The basic necessities are what this visualizes. Bread here stands simply for food, but always, in the Scriptures, this is related also to clothing (Deut. 10:18), to water (Deut. 9:9), to wine (Eccles. 9:7) and to oil (Ps. 104:15). Jesus rejects any sort of greed or unnecessary accumulation.

This daily bread, necessary to one's material life, serves as a basis for another meaning that would also have been in the thinking of the early Christian community. What is the bread needed for spiritual life and humankind's religious dimension? Jesus presents himself as "the bread of life" (John 6:35); "I am speaking of the bread . . . which a man may eat, and never die" (John 6:50); "he shall live forever" (6:51). The bread does not just refer to Jesus. In this daily bread there is also the echo of another bread eaten daily by the Christian community, the Eucharist: "The bread which I will give is my own flesh; I give it for the life of the world" (John 6:51); "whoever eats my flesh and drinks my blood possesses eternal life, and I will raise him up at the last day . . . whoever eats this bread shall live forever" (John 6:54, 58).

These varied meanings have a certain resonance, a vividness of meaning, for the faithful, when they pray: "Give us today our daily bread": primarily it has to do with the material bread without which life cannot continue. This bread points to that bread in the kingdom of God where life will be eternal and happy. The bread of the kingdom has already been anticipated; it is Jesus himself in his life and message. Jesus finds continuity in history in the form of the eucharistic bread, which we have as the anticipatory firstfruits of the kingdom and of the salvation whose outlines have already been traced by Jesus himself. The historical Jesus, the early Christian community, and we ourselves, in today's world, with all our material and spiritual needs, are to be found in this brief but weighty expression: our daily bread.

GIVE US TODAY—HUMAN WORK
AND DIVINE PROVIDENCE

Scripture is full of passages expressing the conviction that it is God who gives bread or food. All nourishment is a divine gift. We should give thanks for it. The first of the table prayers recited by pious Jews begins: "Blessed are you, Lord our God, King of the universe, who feed the whole world by your goodness. By your grace, love, and mercy you give bread to every creature, for your mercy endures forever." Only a pagan or an atheist would not know how to give thanks for daily food. It is in this context that we must understand the petition: *give us* today our daily bread.

But what does it mean, concretely, to ask God for the bread we need? Is it not human labor that puts bread on the table? Jesus recognizes the importance of work. Paul tells us quite realistically: "The man who will not work shall not eat" (2 Thess. 3:10). But human labor is not all that goes into bread. We are dependent on so many predetermined circumstances, in the face of which everyone feels impotent and in the hands of divine providence. It is he who gives us good weather and rain; it is he who gives the strength by which we can do our work; it is he who causes the seed to grow. He is the Lord of creation, a creation that we may modify by our labor but which we cannot produce. In each piece of bread God's hand is more present than is the human hand. Thus believers are quite correct in directing their petition for bread to their Father in heaven.

Furthermore, this petition for bread has an eminently concrete meaning in our own day. There are millions who sort through garbage piles in search of bare necessities. Hundreds of thousands die every year for lack of sufficient bread. The specter of malnutrition and hunger becomes more and more a threat to the entire human race. To these millions of starving persons the plea for bread has a direct, immediate meaning. The words recall, to those whose hunger is satisfied, the admonition of God himself: "Share your food with the hungry" (Isa. 58:7). How bluntly it was put by St. Basil the Great (fourth century):

> The bread that is spoiling in your house belongs to the hungry. The shoes that are mildewing under your bed belong to those who have none. The clothes stored away in your trunk belong to those who are naked. The money that depreciates in your treasury belongs to the poor!

In St. Matthew's version of the prayer the petition is for our bread "today" *(semeron)*; in St. Luke's version it is bread for "each day" *(kat'emeran)*. Both meanings are valid.[93] The first version refers to the immediate sense of the petition: a request for the bread that is needed now, today. The second version refers to the continuing intention of discipleship: asking for the bread that is needed today and every day, thus commending oneself to divine providence.

THE HOLINESS OF BREAD

It is deeply imbedded in human consciousness that bread represents a holy reality. Bread is treated with respect and veneration. Only desacralized societies act otherwise, and it is because they have lost their basic point of reference as to what is holy and sublime for humankind and the world. Bread is holy because it is associated with the mystery of life, which is sacrosanct.

For the person of the Old Testament, bread was one of the primordial signs of the grace and love with which God sustained and surrounded his people. It was what God used to exorcise the demons of hunger and death. For the Christian believer, bread is even more holy because it symbolizes the final reunion of all the just at their banquet with God in the future kingdom. It is also a meaningful symbol of Jesus, the bread of life, who has redeemed us to eternal life. Daily bread is holy for still one other reason: it is the material that, when transubstantiated, constitutes the sacrament of the Eucharist, the bread of pilgrims. It nourishes their life, so that they may be resurrected and experience eternal happiness.

To the word "bread" the mysterious word *epiousios* ("supersubstantial, daily, necessary, future, essential") has been added— a word not found elsewhere in Greek literature. It seems to have been coined by the evangelists, as was recognized by Origen. It may possibly have been coined to express all the secret wealth that is hidden away in the simple reality of bread. The whole spectrum of varied meanings needs to reverberate in the soul of one who would understand this petition and include it in the daily recitation of the Lord's Prayer.

VIII

Forgive Us the Wrong
We Have Done

Lord,
as you look upon those who imprison us
and upon those who deliver us to the torture chamber;
when you consider the actions of our jailers
and the heavy sentences passed upon us by our judges;
when you pass judgment on the life of those who humiliate us
and the conscience of those who reject us,
forgive, O Lord, the evil that they may have done.

Remember, rather, that it was by this sacrifice
that we draw close to your crucified Son:
through torture, we obtain his wounds;
through jail terms, his freedom of spirit;
through punishment, the hope of his kingdom;
through humiliation, the joy of his sons.

Remember, O Lord,
that this suffering germinates, within us,
the crushed seed that sprouts,
the fruit of justice and of peace,
the flower of light and of love.

But remember especially, O Lord,
that we never want to be like them,
or do to our neighbors what they have done to us.
　　　—Brother Fernando, Brother Ivo, and Brother Betto,
　　　"Oração de um prisioneiro" ("Prayer of a Prisoner"),
　　in O Canto na fogueira *("Song from the Execution Pyre"),*
　　　　　　Petrópolis, 1977, p. 346

To be sure, we do not live by bread alone (Matt. 4:4), even though bread is needed. But apart from this minimum infrastructure (food) without which human beings cannot exist or survive, they find themselves caught up in a social fabric that is also an essential part of their very being. In this dimension, one not only lives, but also cohabits, "lives-with." It is here that the human being emerges as a person—that is, as someone capable of relating to others, of listening to or making a proposal, of giving a response to "the other," and of having a sense of responsibility.

To speak of a "person" is to speak of relationships, ties, and alliances that make persons responsible to others, fulfilling them, frustrating them, making them happy or unhappy. As a person, a man or a woman is a responsible being, which also means being responsible to God, either responding to his love or refusing it and withdrawing into a shell. Conscience is the place where one hears the call of "the other" and of God. Freedom brings a person to openness or closedness, to acceptance or refusal of responsibility.

THE EXPERIENCE OF OFFENSE AND INDEBTEDNESS

At the level of relationships, whether to God or to others, various attitudes take shape: love, friendship, sympathy, cooperation, indifference, withdrawal, humiliation, arrogance, exploitation. There is no neutrality here; taking a position is unavoidable: one is either for or against, at varying levels of commitment. The human ego always manifests itself in living with others and committing oneself to them.

Within all this interrelatedness one finds an experience of indebtedness to someone else, or even of reciprocal offenses committed. We feel indebted to others. We did not ask to be born. Once born, there were those who accepted us, fed us, and gave us the care that was indispensable to a healthy life, whereas so many others have been rejected and eliminated.

Religious persons experience something similar in relation to God: they are given existence, health, clothing, the roof over their heads, their intelligence, will to exist, friends, and many excellent things that are a part of life that could not be produced merely by human ingenuity. They experience them simply as a gift from the Father. We see ourselves as debtors; the emotion of thanksgiving arises quite naturally. This might be called an innocent debt, and in a sense it will never be paid. No matter how hard we might try, we shall never repay our debt to the author of life—whether our earthly parents or God.[94] There is a gospel passage that applies here: no matter how much we do to earn gratitude, we are servants and deserve no credit; we have only done our duty (Luke 17:10).

But there is another type of indebtedness that is not so "innocent," a debt of guilt. This is the debt resulting from offenses and sins, a debt that needs to be repaid. Our conscience perceives it as guilt in terms of a relationship that is damaging to human communication, to love, to human nature itself. This offense, or sin, in order to be experienced as such, presupposes a relationship with other persons and a communion with God. What should have been done was not done. Neighbors needed a word from me that would reassure them, and I denied it to them. The sight of them called out for mercy, but I was hardhearted and humiliated them. The poor tell me their troubles and stretch out their hand for help, but I pass by. The eyes of the children glitter with hunger, babies shiver feverishly in the arms of emaciated, undernourished mothers, and I turn away my face in order to keep my composure. On other occasions there has been blind hatred, the overt exploitation of the weak, of one's employees, of someone's ignorance, or physical elimination of troublemakers. Fellowship has been breached and humanity violated. There has been injustice and contempt. A brother or sister was offended. And God has been affected because what pleases him is mercy, love, justice, solidarity—and these have all been betrayed.

We are not giving full expression to this experience if we merely say that a law has been violated. The law commanded me to do to someone else what I should like to have done to me, and I did not do it! Vis-à-vis an abstract law, we do not really feel guilty, but mostly just regret. But what actually happened was a violation of a personal relationship. It was not just a law but a *person* whose dignity was wounded, whose needs were not met; a personal relationship was fractured—not to mention solidarity among all human beings and with God himself. This guilt is most sharply expressed when we feel the call of God and reject it; not a general call but a personal appeal, a vocation that requires commitment of our entire being. A call to fidelity, character development, and growth is not heeded; goods entrusted to our management are buried and yield no gain (see Matt. 25:14–30).

We experience a feeling of responsibility for the offense committed. It did not need to happen, but it did. We experience an indebtedness and the need to ask forgiveness. There is nothing psychopathic or obsessive about this (in such cases the guilt has no real object, and this is what makes it pathological); it is rather a healthy indicator of something that needs to be made right, that requires the restoration of a human relationship that has been violated.[95] Deeply rooted in every person is the awareness that not everything is right in his or her life: "All of us often go wrong" (James 3:2). To be sincere, we have to acknowledge to ourselves that we are sinners; "if we claim to be sinless, we are self-deceived and strangers to the truth" (1 John 1:8). And sin is revealed to the conscience as a debt that needs to be paid. Spontaneous supplication occurs frequently in the Scriptures: Lord, have mercy on us! "In the fullness of thy mercy blot out my misdeeds" (Ps. 51:1). Tormented in conscience, the psalmist cries out: "Look at my misery and my trouble, and forgive me every sin!" (Ps. 25:18). And Sirach suggests that the safest way to obtain forgiveness for our sins is to forgive those who have offended us: "Forgive your neighbor his wrongdoing; then, when you pray, your own sins will be forgiven" (Sir. 28:2). And Jesus says quite matter-of-factly: "Acquit, and you will be acquitted" (Luke 6:37).

Quite apart from this possibility of mutual forgiveness, we sense that we are always in debt. It is not just a matter of renouncing a sinful attitude or of making reparation for an offensive

deed: sin has deeper roots and pervades our whole existence. We
live in a sinful context; the very life-giving air that we breathe has
been polluted, even though God's abiding grace and mercy are
also present.[96] This is why we feel like the victims of the forces of
evil that now and then lead us into sin and into breaking the ties of
fellowship. It is not just a mistake to be corrected but a situation
to be renewed; a new person must come to life. This is what is so
profoundly liberating about the message of Jesus, who is the incarnation of the Father's mercy and forgiveness: "My son, your
sins are forgiven!" (Mark 2:5). The good news of Jesus includes
not only salvation and the genesis of a new heaven and a new earth
inhabited by a renewed humankind, but also the radical and complete remission of all indebtedness and the final forgiveness of all
sin.

FORGIVE US THE WRONG WE HAVE DONE

The observations made above were necessary in order for us to
understand this fifth petition of the Lord's Prayer: "Forgive us
the wrong we have done, as we have forgiven those who have
wronged us." This petition expresses the cry, almost the lament,
of hopelessly sinful humankind, a cry directed to the Father of
infinite mercy.

The Matthean and Lukan versions do not completely agree.
Matthew focuses on "wrongs" or "debts," an expression drawn
from the business world (financial debts) but which with time had
taken on a religious nuance, as a synonym for "offense." The
word "offense" in turn emphasizes the personal nature of sin
which, as we have seen, does not imply simply the violation of a
standard but also the breaking of an interpersonal relationship
that involves God, who is present in every person and in every
human relationship. Luke's text runs: "And forgive us our sins,
for we too forgive all who have done us wrong" (Luke 11:4). Luke
translates "wrongs" or "debts" as "sins" to make it easier for his
readership to understand, because they were Greeks, for whom
"wrongs" or "debts" had none of the religious connotation that it
did for Semites. Nevertheless, in the second part of the petition he
uses the expression "who have done us wrong," where we would
expect "sinners" or "those who sin against us." This reinforces

the conviction that Matthew's version is more original than that of Luke.

We need to reflect on the good news of God's forgiveness, proclaimed and practiced by Jesus. This is the background against which this petition of the Lord's Prayer is uttered.

Jesus' proclamation does not just concentrate on the joyful news that the new heaven and the new earth are about to emerge, whereby total, global liberation is in process and is about to arrive in its fullness. What makes the good news "good" and "happy" is that its first hearers were the poor, the weak, those on the margins of society, and sinners. The Father to whom Jesus bore witness is a father of infinite goodness, who "is kind to the ungrateful and wicked" (Luke 6:35). He is the God of the lamb that strays (Luke 15:1-7), of the lost coin (Luke 15:8-10), and of the prodigal son (Luke 15:11-32). He is the God who rejoices more over one sinner who is converted than over ninety-nine righteous who have no need of conversion (Luke 15:7).

Jesus, who is the incarnation in this world of the Father's mercy, is himself merciful. He practices what he preaches to others: "Be compassionate, as your Father is compassionate" (Luke 6:36). This is why he visits the homes of sinners (Mark 2:15; Luke 19:1-9), to the point where he is regarded as a friend of sinners (Matt. 11:19). This is not a mere humanitarian gesture; it derives from his own experience of a merciful God. Jesus makes sinners feel that they are not automatically excluded from the Father's love, but that the Father loves them with infinite tenderness and that they may accordingly return to his favor. The Father will receive them with open arms and the kiss of pardon (Luke 15:20; 2 Sam. 14:33).

This gospel of mercy was a stumblingblock to some religious persons of Jesus' day, and it continues to scandalize believers even now. Fervent Christians have worked hard to follow the Lord's ways, and so they imagine that because of this they are the only ones whom God loves. Such an attitude transforms them into Pharisees, who treat with harshness the weak and the errant. The principal parables of Jesus dealing with forgiveness and mercy are not directed to sinners but to the pious and those who criticize the prodigal liberality of Jesus and his Father. Jesus' proclamation and merciful practices—allowing himself to be anointed by a well-known prostitute (Luke 7:36–50)—generate criticism. Jesus defends his merciful approach very bluntly: it is not the healthy, but those who are sick, who needed a doctor (Mark 2:17); the Son of Man came to seek and to save what is lost (Luke 19:10); he is sent to the lost sheep of the house of Israel (Matt. 15:24). He speaks provocatively to the religious teachers of his day: the tax collectors and prostitutes (who recognize him) will go into the kingdom of heaven ahead of them (Matt. 21:31) because "you did not change your minds" (Matt. 21:32).

At that time there were three recognized categories of sinners: (1) the Jews who could approach God with repentance and hope; they could count on divine mercy; (2) gentile sinners who could come in repentance but without much hope of being heard; thus they were regarded as outside the reach of God's mercy; and (3) the Jews who became like gentiles; they could count neither on repentance nor on the hope of being heard. For all practical purposes, they were lost. This group included herdsmen, prostitutes, lepers, publicans (tax collectors), and the like.[97] And now these were the ones who were hearing the good news from Jesus: "I did not come to invite virtuous people, but sinners!" (Mark 2:17). To a paralytic belonging to this third group of sinners, Jesus spoke the liberating words: "My son, your sins are forgiven!" (Mark 2:5).

The gospel is understood as good news only if we understand this new idea that Jesus introduced. The God of Jesus is no longer the God of the Torah, the Law. He is the God of mercy, of unlimited goodness, and of patience for the weak who recognize that they are weak and start on the road back to God (Rom. 3:25–26). The parable of the prodigal son gives concrete expression to the God of Jesus Christ, who is full of mercy and overflowing love: "While he was still a long way off, his father saw him and his heart went out to him. He ran to meet him, flung his arms around him, and kissed him" (Luke 15:20). The heavenly Father is like this earthly father. And Jesus is the same in practice.

To justify his own attitude and that of God himself, Jesus supplies his critics with several parables.[98] That of the strayed sheep and the lost coin are addressed to the complaining doctors of the law and the Pharisees (Luke 15:2). That of the two debtors is for Simon the Pharisee (Luke 7:40). The dictum, "It is not the healthy that need a doctor, but the sick," is spoken against the religious specialists, who were the most pious of their day, the Pharisees (Mark 2:16). The parable of the Pharisee and the publican is likewise directed against the Pharisees (Luke 18:9), and so on. In each case, Jesus is seeking to defend the new idea that he has introduced: God is primarily the God of sinners, and the Messiah is he who liberates us from our debts and relieves us of the burden of a heavy conscience.

God's forgiveness knows no limits; it is unrestricted, as is seen in the parable of the servant with a heavy load of indebtedness who requested: "Be patient with me, and I will pay in full" (Matt. 18:26). And he was forgiven the entire debt because he asked, verse 32 tells us. At the same time, we have to understand the full meaning of mercy and forgiveness. They are not automatic or mechanical processes; they presuppose a relationship between the offended and the offender. A person has to seek forgiveness, turn to God and give an account of the embarrassing predicament. Those who regard themselves as righteous, with no sins and with no need for conversion, also see no real need for forgiveness. Unfortunately, they are laboring under false pretenses, not truly aware of the reality of the situation.

This is the illusion of the Pharisee in the parable (Luke 18:9–14) who judges himself to be holy when in fact he is quite hardhearted, "having overlooked the weightier demands of the Law: justice, mercy, and good faith" (Matt. 23:23). In other words, he is a sinner without realizing it. He thinks that he has no reason for requesting forgiveness. He does not ask for it, and therefore he does not receive it. God will forgive, and he is always ready to forgive, but the sinner has to be ready for forgiveness. Otherwise, forgiveness will not be real, and there is no healing of the impaired relationship between God and the sinner. God is merciful, but not overindulgent. When we acknowledge that we are sinners, like the tax collector (who was regarded as a sinner in his day), beat our breast, and say: "O God, have mercy on me, sinner that I am" (Luke 18:13), we may have the assurance of a full pardon and of the fact that the kingdom of God has already taken up residence in our heart.

This unrestricted forgiveness by the Father becomes historical fact when Jesus himself gives unlimited forgiveness to his executioners (Luke 23:34); he freely abandons himself into their hands (Matt. 26:52–54; John 18:8–11). He sees his life as being given to others and to sinners, so that all may be redeemed (Mark 10:45). He takes upon him the predicament of the guilty and prays for God's forgiveness. And God hears and reconciles the world (1 Peter 1:18; Rom. 5:8–10; Acts 8:30–35; Heb. 9:15, 28; Rev. 5:9; 1 Cor. 6:20, 7:23). Residing in him is the full truth that love forgives all (1 Cor. 13:4–7).

Because all this is a reality, we can confidently ask God's forgiveness, as we do in the Lord's Prayer. Through Jesus we know that our petition is heard.

AS WE HAVE FORGIVEN THOSE WHO HAVE WRONGED US

The second part of this petition seems to establish some conditions for divine forgiveness, for it says: "As we have forgiven . . ." (Matthew); "for we too forgive . . ." (Luke). Matthew underscores the correlation. At the end of the Lord's Prayer he adds the words: "For if you forgive others the wrong they have done, your heavenly Father will also forgive you; but if you do not forgive others, then the wrongs you have done will not be forgiven by your Father" (Matt. 6:14–15). Is this a kind of *do ut des* contract? Is it a kind of negotiation with God? The question, thus stated, seems to favor the development of a pharisaical attitude, as though God were requiring something in return. But such would be unworthy of the approach taught by Jesus, which is one of unlimited mercy, completely independent of any selfish considerations.

The parable of the heavily indebted servant (Matt. 18:23–35), who was totally forgiven because he requested it from his master, points us in the right direction. After being forgiven, he did not forgive his fellow servant who owed him a smaller amount. It was then that his master called him and said: "You scoundrel! I remitted the whole of your debt when you appealed to me; were you not bound to show your fellow servant the same pity as I showed you?" (Matt. 18:32–33). The lesson is crystal clear: if we ask for unrestricted pardon and receive it without reservation, subject to no conditions, we shall also have to give unrestricted pardon to someone who asks us for unlimited forgiveness. We are to be merciful as the Father is merciful (Luke 6:36). We must forgive seventy times seven times—that is, without limits (Matt. 18:22)—because this is how God forgives.

Thus there is no business deal here, and there are no strings attached; we are merely expected to maintain the same attitude toward God and toward our neighbor. This is the new element in the experience of God that is communicated to us by Jesus Christ. We cannot maintain two attitudes, one toward God and the other toward our neighbor. Both are subject to a single motivation, that of love. To love "the other" is to encounter God, and to love God implies loving the neighbor, because "if he does not love his brother whom he has seen, it cannot be that he loves God whom he has not seen" (1 John 4:20). Worshiping God without being reconciled with one's neighbor is idolatry (Matt. 5:23–24). The basic commandment, of which Paul reminds us, is: "You must forgive as the Lord forgave you" (Col. 3:13).

Now we can have a full understanding of Jesus' statement: "Acquit, and you will be acquitted" (Luke 6:37); "whatever measure you deal out to others will be dealt back to you" (Matt. 7:2). In other words: if we do not totally forgive our neighbor, then it is a sign that we have not fully requested the Father's forgiveness and we have thus made ourselves incapable of receiving the unrestricted forgiveness of God. If we have really had the radical experience of forgiveness for our sins and our debts, if we truly have felt the mercy of God at work in our sinful life, then we are also impelled to forgive without limits, without reservations, and with a carefree heart. The beatitude applies here: "How blessed are those who show mercy; mercy will be shown to them" (Matt. 5:7). At the end of history and the end of life, only the works of mercy will count; on these depend our salvation or our destruction (Matt. 25:31–46). We have no right to ask God's forgiveness if we do not want to forgive our neighbors.

Finally, as with the previous petition of the Lord's Prayer, we see that this one also has a social dimension.[99] We see ourselves as a community of sinners; we are indebted to God and indebted to our fellow humans. The bread of our communal life is forgiveness and a reciprocal demonstration of mercy; if this is lacking, broken ties cannot be repaired. God's forgiveness reestablishes vertical communion with the Most High; forgiving those who have offended us reestablishes our horizontal communion. The reconciled world begins to flourish, the kingdom is inaugurated, and we begin to live under the rainbow of divine mercy. All this is bound up in the words we pray: "Forgive us the wrong we have done, as we have forgiven those who have wronged us."

IX

And Do Not Bring Us
to the Test

A great spiritual teacher said to his disciple:
   "You cannot trifle with the animal that lives within you without becoming completely an animal.
   "You cannot play with lies without losing your grip on truth.
   "You cannot play cruel games without bruising the tenderness of your spirit.
   "If you want to keep your garden cleared, you cannot allow any room for weeds to grow."

The petitions of the Lord's Prayer grow in intensity until they culminate in this cry of anguish: "Do not bring us to the test!" This request to the Father presupposes a bitter awareness that human beings are fragile, subject to the temptation of betraying their hope, becoming unfaithful to God, actually succumbing to temptation, and consequently being lost. In order to grasp the fundamental meaning of this tormented cry of the soul, we need to become aware of the makeup of the human condition, this being the context into which temptation enters and a breakdown occurs.

THE HUMAN PERSON:
A BEING SUBJECT TO TEMPTATION

The basic orientation of human life incorporates two perspectives, one directed to the earth and the other directed to heaven. Because we live on earth, we share in the earth's fate: frailty, vulnerability, every sort of limitation, and, finally, death. The Scriptures speak of our entire life on earth as life in the flesh; and "flesh-mindedness spells death" (Rom. 8:6).[100] This does not mean that earthly life has no dynamism or relevance; recent centuries have demonstrated the astonishing capacity of humankind to transform nature and society. Science and technology, despite their plundering of the ecosystems, have brought an easier life and a more habitable earth to a considerable percentage of humanity.

In the final analysis, however, we have to ask the question of the ancient wise man: "What reward has a man for all his labor, his scheming, and his toil here under the sun?" (Eccles. 2:22). All our undertakings and achievements are branded with the stigma of mortality, inasmuch as we cannot take charge of everything, we cannot do everything, we cannot become everything. In a word, even the greatest geniuses, the most radical revolutionaries, and the most dedicated protesters have to eat and drink, have to rest and spend time sleeping.

On the other hand, this same humankind that is so restricted lives among the stars, if one considers its desires and impulses. It is not content to resign itself to the pettiness of things; it breaks through all barriers and is always seeking to go beyond defined limits. This is not a question of the will; it is more an innate impulse that causes human beings to hunger for the infinite and thirst for the absolute until one may conclude with Sirach: "When a man has come to the end, he is still at the beginning, and when he has finished he will still be perplexed" (Sir. 18:7). The Scriptures speak of this mode of being as "life in the spirit."[101] The human being in its entirety feels an upward call, toward full freedom, toward final perfection, toward an ultimate resting place. "The spirit alone gives life" (John 6:63) and "spirit-mindedness is life and peace" (Rom. 8:6).

The combination of life in the flesh and life in the spirit comprises the objective structure of human nature. The two are out of balance and cause human life to be torn between them. The human person, ontologically speaking, is an unbalanced being; although confined to limits, we are of unlimited size; though anchored firmly in the ground, we reach up to the stars. What is there to integrate all this? How does this cacophony become a symphony? Paul assures us, quite realistically: "That lower nature sets its desires against the spirit, while the spirit fights against it. They are in conflict with one another so that what you will to do you cannot do" (Gal. 5:17). And all this is found in the single reality we call "human."

These two existential states also constitute two approaches to life. Life is never a "given" or an accomplished fact; it has to be built and guided. Some can establish a lifestyle based on the dimension of the flesh; they are satisfied with what the world can offer, and they repress any suggestions prompted by the spirit. Paul warns us against this type of fundamental choice, because it does not lead to the kingdom of God (Gal. 5:21). This mind-set finds its concrete embodiment in such works as "fornication, impurity, and indecency; idolatry and sorcery; quarrels, a contentious temper, envy, fits of rage, selfish ambition, dissensions, party intrigues and jealousies; drinking bouts, orgies, and the like" (Gal. 5:19–20).

But we shall not content ourselves with generalities. Flesh-mindedness finds its historical expression in contemporary society, with its mechanisms that tend toward the accumulation of wealth in the hands of a few, to the detriment of the large majority, abandoned to poverty and hunger. The social system that predominates in our countries is profoundly inequitable, giving rise to institutionalized injustice and social sin, such as were prophetically denounced at the Puebla conference (*Puebla* 509 and 562). With its seductions and illusions imbedded in the minds of all, it constitutes a permanent collective temptation to selfishness, to insensitivity, and to the violation of fellowship. As a mind-set, it is opposed to life; its fruit is death.

It is also possible to orient life in the spirit dimension. Every manifestation of life (including those of the flesh) are seen as God sees them and from the standpoint of a destiny in which all humans participate more fully. This spirit-mindedness, mentioned in Galatians 5:25, finds its exterior expression in "love, joy, peace, patience, kindness, goodness, fidelity, gentleness, and self-control" (Gal. 5:22). Spirit-mindedness releases life, so that it may blossom. And the Scriptures give the promise: "Choose life, and then you will live" (Deut. 30:19).

Again, it is of importance to give these ideas a historical setting in our own time. All those who are presently committed to nurturing the relationships of production and community living in such a way as to promote community and participation at every level of life, for the largest possible number of persons, are in the process of realizing the designs of the spirit. It is only in such a society that real rather than illusory conditions exist for the emergence of the fruits of the spirit enumerated for us by Paul.

The crisis of the human condition resides in the fact that these two mind-sets are interwoven. The person who chooses spirit-mindedness must battle against the flesh-mindedness that writhes within: "In my inmost self I delight in the law of God, but I perceive that there is in my bodily members a different law fighting against spirit-mindedness and making me a prisoner to the sin-mindedness that is in my members. Miserable creature that I am, who is there to rescue me?" (Rom. 7:22–24).[102]

In order to receive affirmation and support, this spirit-mindedness must confront suffering and testing, both of which are implied in the very concept of faithfulness to this fundamental choice. These testings, despite their painful nature, are charged with meaning: they ratify, strengthen, and purify the fundamental choice. Judith, in her famous speech to the people before she assassinated Holophernes, made a statement that has become a kind of *locus classicus* for this subject: "We have every reason to give thanks to the Lord our God; he is putting us to the test as he did our ancestors. Remember how he dealt with Abraham and how he tested Isaac, and what happened to Jacob. . . . He is not subjecting us to the fiery ordeal by which he tested their loyalty, or taking vengeance on us; it is for discipline that the Lord scourges his worshipers" (Jud. 8:25–27).

Testing, as it is meant here, is the price we pay to be faithful to God. Its real function is not punishment but purification (1 Peter 1:6–7). It is even the subject of a supplication: "Test me, O Lord, and try me; put my heart and mind to the proof" (Ps. 26:2; see also Ps. 139:23). In other places, thanks is given to God for testing: "Bless our God, all nations . . . for thou . . . hast put us to the proof and hast refined us like silver" (Ps. 66:10; see also Isa. 48:10; Sir. 44:20). In the Epistle of James we are asked to regard these testings as "pure joy" (James 1:2). These things crop up in our lives to make the good even better.

All of these anthropological considerations were necessary to help us better understand temptations, which are the subject of this petition of the Lord's Prayer. We need to get beyond a mere moralizing of temptations (which is very superficial) and get into a more structural dimension, where we can see where they are rooted in our human nature. Without this perception we cannot hope to adequately grasp the temptations of Jesus nor the example they are supposed to set for our own life.

The human being, then, is structurally susceptible to temptation, subject both to the solicitations of the flesh and of the spirit. The human being is seen as a passionate being. This is not bad in itself; it only makes us more aware of the overflowing dynamism of our carnal-spiritual humanness. Evil, properly so-called, does not consist in having temptations but in yielding to them. We do not ask God to exempt us from temptation but to protect us when we confront it.

HUMAN NATURE: FRAILTY

The most unfortunate thing about human nature is that it has fallen, and continues to fall, into temptation. Testing, like any crisis (its original meaning being that of cleansing and purification), ceases to be an opportunity for growth and becomes an occasion for failure and denial. Sin denies the love of God, love of neighbor, and of the world, cutting tragically across all human history. And the more we become aware of the excesses of human sin, the more terrifying this tragedy is seen to be. Vatican II stated that "man finds that by himself he is incapable of battling the assaults of evil successfully, so everyone feels as though he is bound by chains" (*Gaudium et Spes* 13).

The great denial has its history and its victims: every person who has come into this world. As far as our salvation is concerned, we are born into a polluted atmosphere. We have been rendered anemic by the historical condition of personal and institutional sin, which increasingly incapacitates us for making our trials into stepping-stones and allows them to degenerate into temptations to unfaithfulness and the denial of our own being.

Righteousness, in its original meaning, signified the ability to integrate all the dynamisms of the flesh and of the spirit into a lifestyle centered upon God, whose offspring we are, on others as our brothers and sisters, and on the world in our capacity as free administrators of earthly goods. Sin has loosened our moorings, so that each impulse flies off in its own direction, disrupting the unity of our humanness.[103]

How is it that the human being can sin, can resist the truth, can become insensitive to community and to love? Could not God have made the human being differently? God is not completely exempt from the tragedy of sin, because, although he is not the author of sin, it occurs by his permission. Although he is omnipotent, he does not prevent sin from happening; he permits it. By faith we know that he permits it, because he knows how to bring a higher good out of evil. But we have not been granted the revelation of this higher good, no matter how much St. Augustine talks about his "blessed guilt"! We eagerly await the glorious revelation of his loving design (see Rom. 8:18). Theology, in its efforts to understand this, seeks to throw some light on this "mystery of iniquity."

In order for sin to exist, the possibility of sin must preexist. And this possibility is connected with the very mystery of creation itself.[104] To speak of creation is to speak of dependence. Every created being is dependent on God for its existence and sustenance; it is from God, is made by God, and exists for God. In comparison with the divine perfection, creation is imperfect. This imperfection is not something evil that we should protest or seek to eliminate. It is the very fact that the world is not God or an intrinsic emanation of God himself (that is, a divine person), that it is separate, different, limited, and dependent. Its ultimate reason for being does not reside in itself but requires Someone to give it meaning. This is an objective situation, an objective description of the structure of created beings.

In the case of human beings, there is an *awareness* of the perfection of God and of the imperfection of the creature. The supreme, infinite reality (God) is out of phase with a contingent, finite reality (the world with all its creatures), and the human spirit is caught between the two realms. Awareness of it takes the form of anxiety and suffering. This anxiety and this suffering cannot be healed by any medicine or therapy. They constitute the ontological structure of the human being and express its dignity as it relates to creation. Only humankind has been raised above other finite beings, and it alone establishes dialogue with the infinite. It alone stands between the finite and the infinite. The human person is not only of the world—although belonging to it—or only of God, even though said to be the image and likeness of God, and "suspended" between God and the world. This fact of belonging to two dimensions of reality causes suffering, for the two realities cut across a person's entire being: flesh (of the world) and spirit (of God), both perfect and imperfect.

This imperfection is quite innocent in itself, and need not cause any major problems. But it constitutes the possibility of testing, of temptation, and of sin. The human person, created and creative, finds this imperfection and finiteness hard to accept, and can very well have the desire to be like God (Gen. 3:5). And what is God like? He is the reality of infinite goodness and love that exists and subsists of itself; he has no need for someone or something else to authenticate his genuineness. God is the Truth, the Good, the Supreme. Human beings, on the other hand, see themselves as creatures permanently subordinated to God. They do not exist by and of themselves; their ultimate raison d'être is not in themselves but in God. Wanting to be like God means desiring the impossible: we can never be like God, because we shall always remain created beings.

Sin is the refusal to accept one's own limitations and the suffering of a spirit enclosed in flesh. This is why sin is always an act of violence against the meaning of creation, which has to be accepted as such. It is an attitude of arrogance (the *hybris* of the Greek tragedies) and is the very height of presumption. This is the true evil, the historical sin, the result of an abuse of freedom. This sin has been accumulating in all human societies and constitutes the sin of the world; it creates mechanisms that become internalized in persons, in lifestyles, becoming like a second nature within men and women.

Thus human society is "passionate" in the pejorative sense of the word; it tempts and solicits to evil. St. James has said it well: "God does not tempt anyone. Temptation arises when a man is enticed and lured away by his own lust" (James 1:13–14). In concrete terms, there exists in each one of us not only a call to altruism, to commitment, and to community, but also a penchant to egotism, to vengeance, and to the instincts of death. We feel righteous and sinful at the same time, both oppressed and liberated. Can we escape this tragic state? Paul asks the question: "Who is there to rescue me out of this body doomed to death?" (Rom. 7:24). And he answers with a sense of relief: "God alone, through Jesus Christ our Lord! Thanks be to God!" (Rom. 7:25). Let us consider how this has come about.

JESUS, HAVING BEEN TEMPTED, CAN HELP THOSE WHO ARE TEMPTED

The testimony of Scripture is explicit in affirming the fact of Jesus' temptation (Mark 1:13; Matt. 4:3, 26:41; Luke 22:28). "Because of his likeness to us he has been tempted in every way" (Heb. 4:15). For since he himself has passed through the test of suffering, he is able to help those who are meeting their test now" (Heb. 2:18). We need to be clear in our understanding of Jesus' temptation. It seems to have had a direct impact on the humanity of Jesus, and indirectly on his divinity, inasmuch as the humanity in him that was tempted was the humanity of God himself. The incarnate God was present in Jesus, and as such he was stripped of his divine attributes and identified with human limitations. This is an essential feature of the mystery of incarnation. The Son did not take upon himself an abstract nature, but the historical, concrete nature of Jesus of Nazareth.

Jesus of Nazareth in his humanity cannot be understood outside this historical framework. The humanity that he assumed was marked by the history of sin; not everything in that humanity was ordained by God's purposes. Paul emphasizes that "God sent his own Son in a form like that of our own sinful nature" (Rom.

8:3). John put it more simply: "the Word became flesh" (John 1:14)—that is, he entered into the darkness of our fallen and rebellious state.

Because he was true man, Jesus partook of the passionate state (in its positive sense) as we have defined it above. In this passionate state there is human flesh-mindedness and human spirit-mindedness. Because he was still a pilgrim and had not reached the eschatological stage, "he too [was] beset by weakness" (Heb. 5:2). Like all wayfarers, he lived in the penumbra of history; not everything was diaphanous and transparent to him; he had room to exercise faith and hope (Heb. 12:2-3). If he was to be made perfect, it had not yet been attained. He lived in an absolute submission to the Father and in total faithfulness to his will. Nevertheless, this will of the Father was to be revealed slowly, as it unfolded. He saw himself as the liberator sent by God, but not every step in the total process of liberation was completely diaphanous.

What steps did the Father want the Son to take? To the degree that Jesus was to perform his mission, he had to have the clear awareness that the kingdom was not to be established through the mediations of political or sacral power or by means of the charismatic and miraculous. The path that he was to take was that of the suffering servant, of the righteous one who abandons himself for the redemption of all sinners.

Jesus' temptations are not to be understood as solicitations to evil or to sin. Because he always lived with his life centered on the Father, this was not a historical possibility. His "temptations" consisted of a constantly faithful search for those concrete steps that would make the will of God a part of history. This meant that Jesus had to solve problems, to deal with deceptions on the part of the people, the Pharisees, and the apostles, and to confront the misunderstandings that culminated in his defamation and persecution.[105] In this sense, Jesus was tempted—put to the test—and he "offered up prayers and petitions with loud cries and tears" (Heb. 5:7). In the Garden of Gethsemane he prayed agonizingly and earnestly (Luke 22:44). The Epistle to the Hebrews makes a very realistic comment: "Son though he was, he learned obedience in the school of suffering" (Heb. 5:8). All obedience is onerous. Jesus was tested by this onus and he triumphed. He could thus serve as an example for those who follow him.

The gospels show a lifelong consistency in Jesus' confrontation with Satan, who is the embodiment of temptation and evil.[106] The Messiah defeated the devil point for point, bringing liberation to all of creation. Thus, immediately after his public appearance for baptism, he was led out into the enemy's camp—the desert—to be tempted there by the seducer (Mark 1:13; Matt. 4:3). The devil was driven off, but he was only marking time (Matt. 8:29), waiting for an opportune moment (Luke 4:13). Jesus gave him no rest and drove him out whenever he met him, whether in the sick or in the hardheartedness of the Pharisees. But he is the *inimicus hominis* who sows tares among the wheat (Matt. 13:25, 39) and enters the heart of Judas (Luke 22:3; John 13:2, 27). He tried to "sift" Simon Peter and the other apostles like wheat (Luke 22:31). Jesus himself asked his apostles to remain with him in his temptations (Luke 22:28). An attack was made during the agony in the Garden of Gethsemane, when Jesus warned his apostles: "Pray that you may be spared the hour of testing" (Luke 22:40). All of Satan's force was let loose at the cross, driving Jesus almost to desperation, so that he cried out: "My God, my God, why have you forsaken me?" (Mark 15:34). But Jesus defeated Satan by committing his spirit, not to the devil, but to the Father (Luke 23:46).

Temptations, then, were not some momentary happening in the life of Jesus but a dark shadow that followed him throughout his life history. The kingdom of God was being built in opposition to the kingdom of evil; evil does not remain idle but makes its iniquity known. Jesus triumphed over the whole history of sin, with its temptations, in his own flesh (Rom. 8:3), and not at some "safe," unreachable distance from the tentacles of tribulation. The greatness of Jesus was not to be found in the absence of temptations, but in his power to overcome all of them.

DELIVER US, LORD, FROM THE GREAT TEMPTATION!

Humanity, and every individual human being, has been exposed to temptation and seduction, and this has been true since the very beginning of human history (Gen. 3) and will be to its very end (Rev. 3:10). When we adhere to Christ and to the community of his followers, we are fortified against the assaults of the world's sin and are transferred to the kingdom of his beloved Son (Col. 1:13; see also Eph. 6:12; Gal. 1:4). Meanwhile, as life goes on, the battle continues and we should "leave no loophole for the devil" (Eph. 4:27).

But the moment will arrive for the great final confrontation— at the very end of the world.[107] This is the "ordeal that is to fall on the whole world" (Rev. 3:10). In the words of Jesus, "as lawlessness spreads, men's love for one another will grow cold" (Matt. 24:12). "Imposters will come claiming to be messiahs or prophets, and they will produce great signs and wonders" (Matt. 24:24; Mark 13:22) and will deceive many because they come with signs of Christ and of holy things. If God would not have compassion on the righteous, "no living thing would survive" (Matt. 24:22). The root of all temptation is that of unfaithfulness to Christ and his kingdom. The terrifying danger of defection and final apostasy runs rampant (2 Peter 2:9).

It is in this context that we hear the anxious prayer of the disciple: "And do not bring us to the test!" But this anxiety is swallowed up in the serenity of someone who has already called upon the Father for the coming of the kingdom and the consummation of his will. We have already known the victory of God through Jesus Christ. We hear his word: "Courage! The victory is mine" (John 16:33) and we know there will be an answer to his prayer: "I pray thee, not to take them out of the world, but to keep them from the evil one" (John 17:15). Despite everything, there is a need to be alert (Mark 13:23) and to ask for perseverance to the end, for only then will we be saved (Mark 13:13).

This petition has a universal eschatological dimension, but it also has an individual, personal dimension. When we die, we will pass through judgment; the most radical crisis of our existence will erupt, with the possibility of a complete purification for life in the kingdom of God. Here the most profound and ultimate decision comes into play, the fruit of all the decisions in our lives as human beings. Our hope may very well be endangered and our trusting commitment can grow weak. The specter of doubt and despair may take shape in our minds. The darkness of life's meaning may possibly bring clouds between us and the Father of infinite goodness, undermining the certainty of the kingdom and throwing doubt upon his will to save us. Then we shall need to make supplication, to cry out: "Do not bring us to the test!"

Save Us from the Evil One

The SS hanged two Jewish men and a youth in front of the whole camp. The men died quickly, but the death throes of the youth lasted for half an hour. "Where is God? Where is he?" someone asked behind me.

As the youth still hung in torment in the noose after a long time, I heard the man call again, "Where is God now?"

And I heard a voice in myself answer: "Where is he? He is here. He is hanging there on the gallows . . ."
The Crucified God (New York: Harper and Row, 1974)
pp. 273–74, citing Elie Wiesel in Night

If the petition "and do not bring us to the test" contains an element of anxiety, the final petition of the Lord's Prayer culminates in a paroxysm, as we cry out to our Father: "but save us from the evil one!" There is now nothing left to ask; it has all been said. To be saved from evil and from the evil one means being ready to enjoy the freedom of the sons of God in the Father's kingdom. When evil has been conquered, the kingdom may come, and the new heavens and the new earth may be inaugurated, where God's name is hallowed and his will is fully done. But evil will have to be conquered, because it is still a persistent part of history and is continually threatening humanity, "like a roaring lion prowling around looking for someone to devour" (1 Peter 5:8).

EVIL AS SITUATION

It is important that we do not minimize our awareness of evil. It is not just some static in the airwaves, some detour of human activity that causes us to arrive late at the goal toward which we strive. It is much more; it is a dynamic thing, a direction taken by history, a design for our lives. Evil, in this sense, has the characteristics of a structure, and this structure organizes a system of transformations that confer unity, consistency, totality, and self-regulation to all the processes that are maintained within the confines of the system.[108]

This structure creates its own scenarios of sin and wickedness; the scenario is made up entirely of elements contained in a backdrop that characterizes a given moment in history. Evil deeds are expressions of predetermined structures and scenarios. We may appropriate these structures and scenarios, may internalize them in our lives, may make them actual life goals, and thus may move into iniquitous, sinful practices. For example, the Puebla conference denounced the capitalist system as a system of sin (no. 92). Due for the most part to this system, "sinful structures" have taken shape on the Latin American continent and give rise to "a grave structural conflict": the increasing wealth of a few running parallel to the growing poverty of the masses (no. 1209).

This system creates its conflict-ridden economic and political scenarios: political repression and labor-union repression, "national security" governments, social crises, and so forth. The political events appearing in the daily newspapers are embodiments of this backdrop. Concrete persons incorporate into their social life this system, which in essence is an exclusivist one, involving the accumulation of wealth and privileges in the hands of a few who bear little social responsibility and become the agents who maintain the system and participate in its injustice.[109] A whole cycle of evil is thus established.

Evil exists in history because there is temptation. And persons fall into temptation; they sin, they betray the promptings of conscience, they disobey the voice of God, which is usually articulated by the signs of the times.[110] This sin creates its own history and its own mechanisms of production. It achieves a relative autonomy; it exercises power over each one of us, to the point that we feel enslaved: "I am the purchased slave of sin. . . . The good which I want to do, I fail to do; but what I do is the wrong which is against my will. . . . I perceive that there is in my bodily members a different law . . . making me . . . a prisoner under the law that is in my members, the law of sin" (Rom. 7:14, 19, 23).

We live in the "sin situation" that St. John calls the sin of the world (John 1:29). It needs to be explained that "the sin of the world" does not mean that the world itself is sin. The world is primarily the good creation of God, for the sake of which the Father sent his beloved Son (John 1:9, 10, 3:16; 2 Cor. 5:19; 1 Tim. 1:15). Creation, however, has been polluted by humankind's historical wrongdoing. "Sin entered into the world" (Rom. 5:12) and, although not completely corrupting the world, it has left deep marks on it (James 1:27). Thus the world as we experience it at present is "enmity to God" (James 4:4), is the source of unhappiness (2 Cor. 7:10) and has not recognized Jesus Christ (John 1:10). Thus "the world" is not to be understood here in a metaphysical but in a historical sense; this world is the symbol of those who are capable of "stifling the truth in their wickedness" (Rom. 1:18), of "spilling the blood of the prophets since the foundation of the world" (Luke 11:50) and of giving support to every sort of hypocrisy and sin (Matt. 23:29–36).

The seriousness of sin lies in the fact that it constitutes a situation or structure. Every situation possesses its degree of independence and objectivity; sin is not just a personal matter, it has an important social and historical dimension. By a situation we mean "that combination of circumstances in which we find ourselves at a given moment; the situation completely envelops us, involves us, makes us a part of the world around us."[111] This situation was not humankind's original destiny, but it has become so. Its destiny was created by the sins of human beings across the whole sweep of history.

These sins did not die with the persons who committed them but have been perpetuated by actions that survived their perpetrators in the form of institutions, prejudices, moral and legal standards, and social customs. A large number of them represent a perpetuatibn of vices, racial and moral discrimination, injustice, against groups of persons and social classes; just becuase someone was born black or poor subjected him or her to a social stigma. This historically created situation becomes a matter of destiny for those born into it: they become victims of the processes by which traditional norms are socialized and internalized—those norms that are so often the bearers of wrongdoing and sin. The person in question has already been categorized, quite apart from his or her own will in the matter or his or her own decisions.

Such persons participate in this process because of the sin of the world; to the extent that they appropriate and accept the situation, the sin of the world grows as their own personal sins are contributed to it. Thus on the one hand they are victims of the sin of the world (because already situated within it), while on the other hand they become agents to reproduce the sin of the world through their own personal sins (by helping to maintain and reanimate the situation).

There is a kind of sinister solidarity in the evil that rankles humankind, throughout history (Rom. 5:12–14, 16). But we must not lose our perspective here: if there is considerable solidarity with the old Adam, there is much more with the new Adam, because "where sin was multiplied, grace immeasurably exceeded it" (Rom. 5:20), and "death established its reign . . . but life shall reign all the more" (Rom. 5:17). But there is no need to emphasize the power of evil; we know that it was so strong that it could do away with the Son of God when he appeared incarnate in human history (John 1:11). And it continues to do away with the other sons of God to this very day.[112]

EMBODIMENTS OF EVIL

Who is behind all this evil? Who really causes wrongdoing? The Scriptures are quite clear on this. There is a spiritual being who is by definition "the tempter" (Matt. 4:3), the "enemy" (Matt. 13:39; Luke 10:19), the great dragon (Rev. 12:9, 20:2), the serpent (2 Cor. 11:3), the one who was a murderer and liar from the beginning (John 8:44; 1 John 3:8), the evil one (Matt. 13:39; Luke 8:12; Acts 10:38), Satan (Mark 3:23, 26, 4:15; Luke 13:16), Beelzebub

(Matt. 12:24, 27; Mark 3:22; Luke 11:15, 18, 19), the prince of this world (John 12:31; 2 Cor. 4:4; Eph. 2:2). Simply stated, he is the evil one, the author of lies, of hatred, of sickness, and of death (Mark 3:23–30; Luke 13:16; Acts 10:38; Heb. 2:14). Human beings who do not deal justly or love their brothers or sisters (1 John 3:10) are seen to be offspring of the devil, as was Cain (1 John 3:12) and Judas Iscariot (John 6:70, 13:2, 27). The tares of Jesus' parable are the children of the evil one, who are opposed to the children of the kingdom (Matt. 13:38)—who *are* the kingdom of God.

How are we to understand this malevolent spiritual being? Is this a being who was created good by God but who, while undergoing a period of testing, fell into rebellion against God, becoming the Evil One by antonomasia? Or is this a literary device, a metaphorical personification representing our experience of being held captive by a widespread evil historically generated by the apostasies of humankind itself? It is an important question in connection with this last petition of the Lord's Prayer. Is "evil" to be understood as the evil one or as "evil" in the abstract? Are we to be delivered from evil (sin, despair, sickness, death) or from the evil one (the devil, Satan)?

There is still some difference among biblical scholars on this point, because there is no satisfactory way of resolving the question on the basis of language analysis.[113] But the great majority understand "evil" as the evil one (Satan, the devil). This final petition intensifies the one immediately preceding it: "do not bring us to the test"—and *especially* (singling out the worst example)—"save us from the evil one."

The context of the Lord's Prayer, as we have mentioned several times already, is apocalyptic and eschatological. At the end of history there will be a great confrontation between Christ and the antichrist, between the children of the kingdom and the children of the evil one (Matt. 13:37–40). Christ and the antichrist will deploy all their forces. Human beings, historically weak and sinful, will run a most serious risk; they will be able to apostatize and fall into the snares of the devil. In this context, believers will pray from the depth of their being and with great anxiety: "Father, save me from the evil one, when he appears!" Paul well said: God the Father "has rescued us from the domain of darkness and brought us away into the kingdom of his dear Son" (Col. 1:13).

If the exegetes choose to interpret "evil" as "the evil one," this does not mean that the problem as to the existence of the evil one (Satan, the devil) has been theologically settled. It is not enough to establish that the evil one is clearly mentioned in the Scriptures. One has to inquire as to the theological content of this expression. Does it have to do with a spiritual being or with a literary embodiment of the prevalence of evil? On this point, more than a serious exegesis is required; there needs to be reflection at the epistemological and theological levels.

We know that the question of demons has been the subject of heated discussion among theologians.[114] Not a few theologians tend to grant only a symbolic existence to the demons. It is good for us to ponder the words of the respected Catholic exegete, Rudolph Schnackenburg:

> There is a new relevance to the question of whether it is necessary to understand Satan (having eliminated mythological and "humanized" conceptions of him) as a personal spiritual power or merely as the incarnation of evil, inasmuch as this evil is present in history and dominates it through human activities. Today we would not defend the first option with the same certainty as in the past. The demythologization debate counsels caution. The problem of how far one may and should interpret, in line with our present state of knowledge, the affirmations of the New Testament, being bound as they are to a worldview no longer held, is very difficult and cannot be answered by just one exegete. And this has relevance also to the discussion that has now been rekindled concerning angels and demons. The diversity of statements, the stylistic forms previously fashioned, the multiple sources of our ideas concerning Satan, the demons, and the "powers," all converge to indicate that in all this we are not dealing with modes of expression that should not be interpreted literally, as though they had no real substance.[115]

This position gives evidence of intellectual honesty in the face of investigations by exegetical science, and at the same time an awareness of the difficulty of resolving the problem by recourse to this science alone. We do not expect to decide the question here.[116] We only want to call attention to the fact that it is characteristic of religious thought the world over not to find the expression of evil in abstract principles but in living forces, whether benevolent or malevolent, which take on an objective metaphysical reality.[117] Evil has never been experienced in a vague, abstract form, nor have grace and goodness. We are always dealing with concrete situations, whether favorable or unfavorable, with the destructive or constructive historical forces of human relationships, of decent, comradely relationships, with ideologies of power and domination, or with those of cooperation and participation, with concrete bearers in the form of groups or of persons who embody these ideologies in their practical social life. Evil has a definite physiognomy, even though it may be concealed behind masks and disguises.

In the Old Testament, for example, there are incarnations of political powers that rise up against God and his holy people: Gog and Magog (Ezek. 38) or the "little horn" and the fourth beast of the Book of Daniel (7:7, 8), which probably represents the Syrian empire of Antiochus Epiphanes (175–164 B.C.) under whom the people of Israel were cruelly oppressed (Dan. 7:25). The apocalyptic environment has given us a "theology of the tyrant of the end times" as the last great adversary of God. The New Testament projects the figure of the antichrist (2 Thess. 2:1–12; Rev. 13:1–11; 1 John 2:18, 19, 4:3; 2 John 7). He experiences a *parousia* similar to that of Christ and is surrounded by a community of evildoers (2 Thess. 2:9–11; Rev. 13:8). Christ incarnates the mystery of piety (1 Tim. 3:16); the antichrist embodies the mystery of iniquity (2 Thess. 2:7).[118]

Religious metaphysics, with its tendency to concretization, hypostatizes these realities within a supernatural framework. This is its vocabulary and the grammar of the expression of its workings. Theological understanding, for its part, seeks to get beyond the pictures and, so far as possible, to identify the realities and the ideas pertaining to them. Although seeming to desacralize them, it seeks to understand them as intrahistorical realities, manifestations of human wickedness that become embodied in collective forces and representations, against whom mere individuals find it difficult to protect themselves. The evil one would then simply be the organization of injustice, or humankind's departure from its essential calling, the aberration that becomes historically stratified and is forever opposed to the spirit of God, of justice, of goodness—in a word, to the realities of the kingdom.

We may assume that psycho-social development does not move inexorably in the direction of a growth in truth, concord, community, and the participation of everyone in the whole of life, but toward the exasperation that comes from contradictions. In this type of representation, the end of the world will signify an immense process of catharsis, a purifying crisis, at the end of which God will triumph and will lead history on to a transhistorical stage. *Et tunc erit finis*—and then it will be over. That is, the end will then come, and with it a new beginning: there will be an end to this dialectical type of history, and a new phase of history will be inaugurated, a movement toward God for which human beings have anxiously hoped. The Christian faith expresses this truth in its symbolic vocabulary: "The Lord Jesus will destroy the lawless one with the breath of his mouth, and annihilate by the radiance of his coming" (2 Thess. 2:8).

JESUS AND THE VICTORY OVER EVIL

There is a profound and solid conviction in the New Testament to the effect that Jesus is the great deliverer from the power of Satan.[119] According to the mythology of that day, all diseases and infirmities are manifestations of the power of Satan. He holds humanity captive, so that it is subject to every sort of tribulation. But now one who is stronger has arisen to conquer the "strong man" (Mark 3:27).

Jesus accepts the religious metaphysics of the time. He understands Satan as a force in history (the *dynamis* of Luke 10:19) with an organization like that of an army of soldiers (Mark 5:9; Matt. 10:25). He himself is aware that the end of Satan's power is at hand: "If it is by the finger of God that I drive out the devils, then be sure the kingdom of God has already come upon you" (Luke 11:20).

The kingdom of God is being built in opposition to the kingdom of this world, and it inflicts damage on the evil one

(Mark 1:23-25, 39, 4:39; Luke 13:16).[120] Each time demons are driven out, one more degree of victory over him has been achieved, in anticipation of his final destruction. This victorious power is conferred upon the disciples (Mark 6:7; Matt. 10:8; Luke 10:19). When the seventy-two disciples came back jubilant from their mission, saying: "In your name, Lord, even the devils submit to us," Jesus entered into their joy and said: "I watched how Satan fell, like lightning, out of the sky" (Luke 10:17-18). Jesus had a vision; in the annihilation of Satan's power he saw the state of paradise emerging, where humankind is to be reconciled with nature, for "nothing will ever harm you" (Luke 10:19).

As important as this perspective is in the gospels, we must not allow it to get out of focus. For Jesus, this focus is not so much the victory over the evil one as the proclamation of the good news of God's plan of salvation, especially for the defenseless, the poor, the lowly. It is the healings more than the victories over the diabolical dimension of life that manifest the presence of the kingdom, of the new order that God desires, and the inauguration of the new age. Thus the apostles are blessed in that they see what many prophets and kings desired to see and did not (Luke 10:23-24; Matt. 13:16-17).

As a consequence, Jesus' followers do not begin by requiring renunciation of the devil, as the Essenes of Qumran did, but what he asks of them is adherence to the kingdom. In his exhortations he does not warn them to beware of uncontrollable and diabolical forces, but to beware of the yearnings of their own hearts, for these are what corrupt a person's life (Mark 7:15). What keeps someone from entering the kingdom and experiencing the transcendent meaning of life is not so much the devil as wealth (Luke 6:24-25, 12:13, 21, 16:13), excessive worries (Matt. 6:19-34), a self-centered attitude (Mark 9:43-48), passing judgment on others (Matt. 7:1-5), lusting for power, honor, and glory (Mark 10:35-45), an exaggerated, sterile piety (Mark 11:15-19), gullibility (Mark 13:5-7), and the temptation to abuse the good faith of others (Mark 9:42; Matt. 18:6; Luke 17:1-3).[121]

The principal cause of the world's ills is to be found in our insensitivity, our lack of solidarity, and the failure to love. It is this that Jesus criticizes in the Pharisees (Matt. 23:23). These are the real demons that we must exorcise from our lives. When this is accomplished, the grace of God is seen to be victorious in the world. To follow Jesus, which is the central theme of the gospels, calls for creating this new mentality, a truly liberated attitude. "If God is on our side, who is against us?" (Rom. 8:31).

THE FINAL CRY OF THE HUMAN HEART: SAVE US, FATHER!

The Greek term used in the Lord's Prayer for "save" is *rysai*. Its original sense differs from that of the Latin *liberare* or the English "liberate." The common meaning of "liberation" presupposes an experience of captivity, of being in chains and oppressed. This meaning could be verified here, inasmuch as the presence of sin and the evil one imposes slavery on human life. And God has been revealed as a liberator (Ps. 18:2, 40:17, 70:5, 144:2; Dan. 6:27). His liberating action has been conveyed in St. Jerome's Vulgate by the term *liberare* (about two hundred times).[122] For instance, a truthful witness *saves* lives (Prov. 14:25); the Israelites are *liberated* from Egyptian captivity (Exod. 3:8, 14:30, 18:10).

But the original meaning of the Greek *ruesthai* is that of snatching a person away from the brink of an abyss, protecting someone from the vicissitudes of a journey, protecting someone from the traps that lie in the path. As we read in the Psalms: "Keep me from the trap which they have set for me. . . . Let the wicked fall into their own nets, while I pass in safety" (Ps. 141:9–10); "let no flood carry me away, no abyss swallow me up" (Ps. 69:15); "he himself will snatch you away from fowler's snare or raging tempest" (Ps. 91:3).

The underlying experience is that of life as a pilgrimage, as a covenant with God to walk in his paths. Along this path we experience dangers of every kind; there are yawning abysses, there are traps laid by enemies, and we can be attacked. Within the framework of this figurative language, what does the evil one do? His task is to tempt us, to draw us away from the good path, to give us wrong directions. And what does God do? God protects us from the dangers, pulls us away from the ambushes, and shows us the right direction to travel. God said to Jacob: "I will be with you, and I will protect you wherever you go and will bring you back to this land; for I will not leave you until I have done all that I promised" (Gen. 28:15). In Isaiah, he says: "Thus says the Lord, your ransomer . . . I lead you in the way you must go" (Isa. 48:17). And the same prophet asks God in a rather complaining tone: "Thou, Lord, art our father . . . our Ransomer from of old. . . . Why, Lord, dost thou let us wander from thy ways?" (Isa. 63:16–17).

What are these ways or paths of God? They are the ways or paths that lead us toward justice, truth, and fellowship, overcoming the forces of selfishness and oppressive power. As may be seen from the above texts, "saving," "liberation," or "deliverance" is found in the context of a "pilgrimage," a "journey," and of the dangers that go with it, a trek that leads either toward the realization of human desires or toward their frustration.

Each generation has its own "evil one" against which it must particularly protect itself and because of which it must implore divine protection. This evil being embodies the widespread wickedness that permeates humanity. In our own time, the evil one who offends God and debases human persons appears in the form of a collective selfishness embodied in an elitist, exclusivist social system that has no solidarity with the great multitudes of the poor. He has a name; he is the Capitalism of private property and the Capitalism of the state. In the name of money, privileges, and the reinforcement of governmental structures he holds men and women in terror. Many of them are imprisoned, tortured, and killed. Two-thirds of the population are held prisoner under the yoke of a legion of demons: hunger, sickness, disintegration of the family, and a shortage of housing, schools, and hospitals. This evil one has his ways of tempting; he slyly creeps into our minds and makes the heart insensitive to those structural inequities that he has created.

In the context of apocalyptic eschatology the evil one directly named in this petition of the Lord's Prayer assumes that humanity is drawing close to its final destination. Emerging all along this final leg of the journey are the many obstacles, the many gaping abysses, and the danger of defection from the undertaking that is about to achieve its goal. In the midst of this distressing situation the believer and the believing community cry out: "Father, save us from the evil one and from all evil! As you have not allowed us to fall into temptation, now snatch us away from the maneuverings of the evil one!" But the danger does not beckon only at the end of history; it is part of the structuring of the present; it lurks in every corner and seeks to destroy us. And so we cry out to the Father: "Save us from evil! Protect us from moving away from the dimension of goodness. Father, do not let us forsake you!"

If we have prayed from the depths of our hearts, then our confidence can be restored, because it is Jesus who has given us his guarantee: "If you ask anything in my name, I will do it" (John 14:14); "courage! The victory is mine; I have conquered the world" (John 16:33); "stand upright and hold your heads high, because your liberation is near" (Luke 21:28).

XI

Amen

Our Father in heaven
—and your name is holy—
why is your will not done
on earth as in heaven?

Why do you not give all of us
our daily bread?

Why do you not forgive our wrongs
that we might forget our complaints?
Why do we still yield to the temptation to hate?

Our Father, if you are in heaven,
why do you not save us from this evil
so that we may then say Amen?
—Marialzira Perestrello, prayer,
in Ruas Caladas *(Rio de Janeiro, 1978), p. 59*

The Lord's Prayer ends as it ought to end: with a resounding amen. The Hebrew word *amen* has its root in the verb *'mn,* which also forms a part of Hebrew words referring to faith, truth, assurance, firmness, and confidence. To have faith, biblically, means more than holding to certain truths; it also implies a serene trust in

121

a mysterious, ultimate sense of reality. We can say to the world, to life, to everything that exists: amen, so be it! This is why the opposite of faith is fear, and the inability to entrust oneself confidently to a greater power. This greater power, whom we sense as being mysterious and ultimate, the meaning behind all meanings, is discerned as God, the Father of infinite goodness and love. Thus amen signifies: So be it! Yes, may it be so! The amen reinforces, confirms, and reaffirms a petition, a prayer, or an offering of praise (Rom. 1:25, 11:36; Gal. 1:5; Phil. 4:20; 1 Cor. 16:24).[123]

Being able to say amen implies being able to trust and be confident and certain that everything is in the hands of the Father; he has already conquered mistrust and fear, despite everything. The Lord's Prayer has encompassed the whole path of humanity in its drive toward heaven and its rootage in the earth. One finds in it the motif of light and the motif of darkness. And to all of it we say "Yes, so be it!" And we can say yes and amen to the threat of evil, to the promptings of temptation, to the insults we receive, and to the onerous quest for bread, only if we retain our certainty that God is our Father, that we are consecrated to his holy name, that we are confident that his kingdom will come, and that we are sure his will is to be done on earth as it is in heaven.

The Lord's Prayer begins with the confidence of those who lift their eyes heavenward, whence comes our deliverance. After passing through human oppressions, we end with the same confidence and pray amen. This confidence finds its starting point in Jesus himself, who is the one who taught us to pray the Lord's Prayer. He has taken upon himself all the contradictions of our dialectical existence and delivers us from them totally.

St. Paul communicates this with telling insight: "With him it was, and is, Yes" (2 Cor. 1:19). Everything that God has promised to us—and the Lord's Prayer sums up the promises of God, both for life eternal and for life here on earth—"is Yes in Jesus" (2 Cor. 1:20). St. John speaks of Jesus apodictically as "the Amen" (Rev. 3:14).[124]

If Jesus is the Amen that we add to our petitions, then we have the greatest certainty imaginable that God always hears us. Greater than the certainty of our needs is the certainty of our confidence in knowing that our Father looks after us. Amen.

Notes

1. A deeper and more detailed treatment of this subject can be found in Leonardo Boff, "O pensar sacramental, sua estrutura e articulação," *Revista Eclesiástica Brasileira (REB)* 35 (1975): 515–40.
2. For an English translation of the final document of Puebla, see *Puebla and Beyond*, ed. John Eagleson and Philip Scharper, trans. John Drury (Maryknoll, N.Y.: Orbis, 1979).
3. See Leonardo Boff and Clodovis Boff, *Da libertação: O sentido das libertações sócio-históricas* (Petrópolis: Vozes, 1979).
4. See Joachim Jeremias, *O pai-nosso: A oração do Senhor* (São Paulo, 1976), p. 56; Eng., *The Lord's Prayer*, trans. John Reuman (Philadelphia: Fortress, 1964).
5. These have been translated into French from Greek and Latin by Adalbert Hamman, *Le Pater expliqué par les Pères* (Paris: Ed. Franciscaines, 1952).
6. For prayer in general, see the classic work of Friedrich Heiler, *Das Gebet: Eine religionsgeschichtliche und religionspsychologische Untersuchung*, 5th ed. (Munich-Basel, 1959); Eng., *Prayer: A Study of the History and Psychology of Religion*, trans. and ed. Samuel McComb with J. Edgar Park (New York: Oxford University Press, 1932, 1958). For Christian prayer, the best study available so far, see Adalbert Hamman, *La Prière*, 2 vols. (Paris: Desclée, 1963).
7. Tertullian, *De oratione*, P.L. 1, 1153. See H. van den Bussche, *Understanding the Lord's Prayer*, trans. Charles Schaldentrand (New York: Sheed & Ward, 1963), pp. 13–14.
8. See Charles Moeller, *L'homme moderne devant le salut* (Paris: Ed. Ouvrières, 1965); Eng., *Man and Salvation in Literature*, trans. Charles Quinn (Notre Dame, Ind.: University of Notre Dame Press, 1970); idem, "Aspectos do ateísmo na literatura moderna," in *Deus está morto?* (Petrópolis: Vozes, 1970), pp. 281–302; G. Greschake, "Leiden

und Gottesfrage," *Geist und Leben* 50 (1979): 102-21, with many examples, esp. pp. 101-17.

9. In a discussion on the Lord's Prayer, in *Experiências* (Petrópolis: Vozes, 1970), pp. 192-94, Toynbee argues in this way: If God is omnipotent he can do everything. If he can do everything, why does he not eliminate evil? If he does not eliminate evil, he is either not omnipotent or he is not good. Goodness and omnipotence are mutually exclusive. If they could be joined, it would mean that God is God and also the devil (p. 193). We will see in due course how to overcome this false alternative: God is so omnipotent that he can tolerate evil without being defeated by it.

10. Stoicism was the school of philosophy and the way of wisdom that advocated fatalism vis-à-vis the world; it counseled adjustment to and insertion into the principle of reality and called for a certain titanism in the sense of bearing and suffering everything with serenity and magnanimity. This ideal even now attracts certain spirits, a Freud or a Toynbee among many others. It always remains an open question: Can a human being trust only in himself or herself and their own forces? Are there not demands made on human nature that, left to itself, normally bring it to disaster? Or is it not that the human being is called to yield to a Greater and repose in it? See the excellent reflections on this by Otto Kuss, "Zur Vorschungsglauben im Neuen Testament," in *Auslegung und Verkündigung*, vol. 2 (Regensburg, 1966), pp. 139-52, esp. 139-46.

11. See Leonardo Boff, "O projeto histórico de Jesus," *Paixão de Cristo, paixão do mundo* (Petrópolis: Vozes, 1978), pp. 21-38.

12. See F. J. Schierse, "Die Krise Jesu von Nazareth," in *Christentumals Krise*, by various authors (Würzburg, 1971), pp. 35-65, esp. pp. 38-41.

13. See the classic work on this interpretation, which provoked enormous discussion then and still does: J. Weiss, *Die Predigt Jesu vom Reiche Gottes* (1892), 2nd ed. (Göttingen, 1900); Albert Schweizer, *Geschichte der Leben-Jesu-Forschung* (1906), 2 vols. (Hamburg, 1966), esp. vol. 2, pp. 402-51, 620-30; Eng., *The Quest of the Historical Jesus: A Critical Study of the Progress from Reimarus to Wrede*, trans. W. Montgomery (New York: Macmillan, 1961). In our interpretation of the Lord's Prayer, we hereafter take up the Catholic perspective of Otto Kuss and the Protestant one of Ernst Lohmeyer; see the following note.

14. The principal reference works that we will be using in our reflections are the following: Oscar Dibelius, *Das Vaterunser: Umrisse zueiner Geschichte das Gebets in der Alten und Mittleren Kirsche* (Giessen, 1903); Ernst Lohmeyer, *Das Vater-unser* (Zurich: Vanderhoeck & Ruprecht, 1952); Eng., *The Lord's Prayer*, trans. John Bowden (London:

Collins, 1965); Joachim Jeremias, *Abba: Studien zur neutestamentlichen Theologie und Zeitgeschichte* (Göttingen: Vanderhoeck & Ruprecht, 1966), esp. pp. 15-57 (*The Prayers of Jesus* includes chaps. 1, 2, and 4 of *Abba: Studien* [Philadelphia: Fortress, 1978]; see also Part 3, "The Lord's Prayer in the Light of Recent Research"); Otto Kuss, "Das Vater-unser," in *Auslegung und Verkündigung*, vol. 3 (Regensburg, 1966), pp. 277-333; A. Hamman, "La prière du Seigneur," *La Prière*, vol. 1 (Tournai: Desclée, 1959), pp. 94-134; W. Marchel, *Abba, Père: La prière du Christ et des chrétiens* (Rome, 1963); H. van den Bussche, *Le notre Père* (Brussels, 1960); Eng., *Understanding the Lord's Prayer*, trans. Charles Schaldenbrand (New York: Sheed & Ward, 1963); T. Soiron, *Die Bergpredigt Jesu* (Fribourg, 1941), pp. 314-70; L. Sabourin, *Il vangelo di Matteo: Teologia e Esegesi* (Rome, 1976), pp. 425-57; and others in our Bibliography.

15. Kuss, "Das Vater-unser," pp. 279-80; Lohmeyer, *The Lord's Prayer*, pp. 15-20 and passim.

16. See the retranslation made by Jeremias, *The Prayers of Jesus*, p. 94.

17. The *Didache*, 8, 2, calls for the recitation of the Lord's Prayer three times a day. The *Didache* is dated between A.D. 50 and 70; see J. P. Audet, *La Didachè: Instructions des Apôtres*, Etudes Biblique (Paris: Gabalda 1958); Eng., *The Didache*, trans. James A. Kleist, in Ancient Christian Writers, no. 6 (Westminster, Md.: Newman, 1948).

18. Jeremias, *The Prayers of Jesus*, p. 89.

19. See the parallels done by Hamman, *La Prière*, vol. 1, pp. 98-99. The Shemoneh Esre was for the Jews prayer par excellence; many of the eighteen benedictions are from the first half of the first century, the rest may go back to earlier times. A final form was made of them in the 90s under Gamaliel II: Paul Billerbeck and Herman Strack, *Kommentar zum neuen Testament aus Talmud und Midrash* (Munich: Beck, 1922-1961), IV, pp. 208-49, cf. I, p. 407. The Qaddish is dated in the 600s, C.E.

20. Jeremias, *The Prayers of Jesus*, pp. 89-91.

21. See Lohmeyer, *The Lord's Prayer*, p. 13; Kuss, "Das Vater-unser," p. 280.

22. Tertullian, *De oratione*, P.L. 1, 1153.

23. See Jeremias, *Abba*, pp. 15-66; idem, *The Prayers of Jesus*, pp. 29-65; idem, *Neutestamentliche Theologie: Die Verkündigung Jesu* (Gütersloh: Mohn, 1971); Eng., *New Testament Theology: The Proclamation of Jesus*, trans. John Bowden (New York: Scribner's, 1971), pp. 61-67; Lohmeyer, *The Lord's Prayer*, pp. 314-18; W. Marchel, *Dieu-Père dans le Nouveau Testament* (Paris: Cerf, 1966); idem, *Abba, Père*, pp. 101-77; A. Merad, A. Abecassis, and D. Perezil, *N'avons-nous pas le*

même Père? (Le Chalet, 1972), pp. 111–29; F. J. Schierse, "O pai de Jesus," *Mysterium Salutis* II/I (Petrópolis: Vozes, 1972), pp. 84–85.

24. See Paul Ricoeur, "Fatherhood: From Fantasy to Symbol," trans. Robert Sweeney, *The Conflict of Interpretations: Essays in Hermeneutics*, ed. Don Ihde (Evanston, Ill.: Northwestern University Press, 1974), pp. 468–97, esp. pp. 487–88; Marchel, *Dieu-Père*, pp. 33–34.

25. See Gregory of Nyssa (died 394), *De Dominica oratione*, P.G. 44, 1136–1148, trans. Hamman, *Le Pater expliqué*, p. 114: "It is clear that no levelheaded person would use the name of father unless he or she recognized some likeness to him."

26. See the wealth of examples in the classic works: Heiler, *Prayer*, pp. 74–103; Gerardus van der Leeuw, *Phänomenologie der Religion* (Tübingen, 1933); Eng., *Religion in Essence and Manifestation: A Study in Phenomenology*, 2 vols., trans. and ed. J. E. Turner (New York: Harper Torchbook, 1963; reprint, Gloucester, Mass.: Peter Smith, 1967), vol. I, pp. 177–80; H. Tellenbach, ed., *Das Vaterbild in Mythos und Geschichte* (Stuttgart-Berlin: Kohlhammer, 1976).

27. Hamman, *La prière*, vol. 1, p. 82.

28. *Iliad*, iv, 235, v, 33, xii, 631; cf. *Odyssey*, xiii, 128, xx, 112.

29. Aristotle, *Politics*, I, 12.

30. Jeremias, *Abba*, p. 15; idem, *Abba, Jésus et son Père* (Paris: Seuil, 1972), p. 9.

31. Certainly the following passages: Deut. 32:6; 2 Sam. 7:14, 1 Chron. 17:13, 22:10, 28:6; Ps. 68:8, 89:27; Isa. 63:16 (twice), 64:7; Jer. 3:4, 19, 31; Micah 1:6, 2:10. God compared with an earthly father: Deut. 1:31, 9:5; Ps. 103:13; Prov. 3:12. The idea of God as Father is preserved in many personal names in Israel; e.g., Abi-ram (My Father is lofty), Abi-ezer (My Father is help), Abi-yah (My Father is Yahweh), Abi-tub (My Father is goodness); see Albert Gelin, *Les idées maîtresses de l'Ancien Testament* (Paris: Cerf, 1950); Eng., *Key Concepts of the Old Testament*, trans. George Lamb (New York: Sheed & Ward, 1955), p. 33.

32. See C. Vriezen, *Theologie des Alten Testaments in Grundrissen* (Neukirchen, n.d.), pp. 118–22.

33. Cf. this other text, Isa. 64:8: "But now, Lord, thou art our father, we are the clay, thou the potter, and all of us are thy handiwork."

34. Origen in his *De oratione* (P.G. 11, 485–549) recognizes this: "In the Old Testament there exists no prayer invoking God in the name of Father"; cf. Hamman, *Le Pater expliqué*, p. 50: "Now God is invoked in this sense by reason of that complete confidence that the Savior has transmitted to us." Jeremias has found confirmation of the fact that in the Old Testament and in later Palestinian Judaism there is no personal invocation, "My Father": *Abba, Studien*, pp. 19–33, *Abba, Jésus et son Père*, p. 26.

35. See the documentation in Jeremias, *Abba, Studien*, pp. 62–63; idem, *New Testament Theology*, p. 66; idem, *The Prayers of Jesus*, pp. 97–98.

36. Jeremias, *The Prayers of Jesus*, p. 97.

37. For the exegesis of these passages, see Lohmeyer, *The Lord's Prayer*, pp. 38–44.

38. See Ricoeur, *Conflict of Interpretations*, p. 490: "It is on the basis of this category that we must interpret the category of fatherhood. Eschatological royalty and fatherhood remain inseparable, right into the Lord's Prayer; this begins with the invocation of the Father and is continued by the 'petitions' concerning name, kingdom, and will, which are understandable only in the perspective of an eschatological fulfillment. Fatherhood is thus placed in the realm of hope. The Father of the invocation is the same as the God of the preaching of the kingdom, which one enters only if one is like a child."

39. Leonardo Boff, "Filhos no Filho," *A graça libertadora no mundo* (Petrópolis: Vozes, 1976), pp. 220–30; Eng., *Liberating Grace*, trans. John Drury (Maryknoll, N.Y.: Orbis Books, 1979), pp. 184–92.

40. See Lohmeyer, *The Lord's Prayer*, pp. 57–62.

41. St. Gregory of Nyssa in his commentary on the Lord's Prayer (P.G. 44, 1136–1148) (translation by Hamman, *Le Pater expliqué*, pp. 116–17) has good comments on heaven as fatherland. St. Ambrose, commenting on the Lord's Prayer (P.L. 16, 450–454) says in regard to heaven, "Heaven is where there is no fatal wounding"—*uni nullum mortis est vulnus*.

42. See the lucid study of Ricoeur, "Religion, Atheism, Faith," in, *Conflict of Interpretations*, pp. 440–67; and also Louis Evely, *We Dare to Say Our Father* (New York: Herder & Herder, 1965; Doubleday, 1975), pp. 22–43.

43. The famous work of A. Mitcherlich treats of this, *Auf dem Weg zur vaterlosen Gesellschaft* (Munich, 1963); a presentation and critique of this book has been done by M. Juritsch, *Sociología da paternidade* (Petrópolis: Vozes, 1970), pp. 134–41. We highly recommend this book on the anthropology of paternity in an interdisciplinary dialogue.

44. Juritsch, *Sociología*, p. 137.

45. See the important effect of C. G. Jung, *Die Bedeutung des Vaters für Schicksal des Einzelnen* (Zurich, 1949).

46. Rubem Alves, *O enigma da religião* (Petrópolis: Vozes, 1976); the whole first part is dedicated to a discussion of critiques of Freud, Marx, Nietzsche, and others.

47. See Friedrich Nietzsche, *Beyond Good and Evil: A Philosophy for the Future*, translated by Walter Kaufman (New York: Random House, 1966); and *On the Genealogy of Morals*, translated by Walter

Kaufman (New York: Random House, 1967).

48. See the work of J. M. Pohier, *Au nom du Père* (Paris, 1972), where he discusses the principal themes of Christian faith within the framework of the questions raised by Freud.

49. See the judicious statements of Ricoeur, *Conflict of Interpretations*, pp. 470–73.

50. See the reflections of C. Surian, *Elementi per una teologia del desiderio e la spiritualità di San Francesco d'Assisi* (Rome, 1973), pp. 113–15.

51. See the exposition in Leonardo Boff, *O rostro materno de Deus* (Petrópolis: Vozes, 1979).

52. See St. Cyprian, *De oratione*, P.L. 4, 521–38, in the translation by Hamman, *Le Pater expliqué*, p. 27.

53. Tertullian, P.L. 1, 1153–1165; translation by Hamman, *Le Pater expliqué*, pp. 16–17.

54. See the collection of these expressions in Hamman, *La Prière*, vol. 1, pp. 172–83.

55. Origen, in his commentary on the Lord's Prayer, observes that this supplication presupposes that the name of the Father has not yet been sanctified; *De oratione*, P.G. 11, 489–549; translation by Hamman, *Le Pater expliqué*, p. 58.

56. St. Francis warned his confreres not to count up or recount the miseries of this world so as not to question God or blaspheme his name.

57. See Santo de Fraine, in *Dicionário Enciclopédico da Bíblia* (Petrópolis: Vozes, 1971), pp. 1389–93; one of the more detailed studies, by Otto Procksch and Karl George Kuhn, can be found in *Theologisches Wörterbuch zum Neuen Testament*, ed. Gerhard Kittel (Stuttgart: Kohlhammer, 1957), vol. 1, pp. 87–116; Eng., *Theological Dictionary of the New Testament*, ed. Gerhard Kittel, trans. and ed. Geoffrey W. Bromiley (Grand Rapids, Mich.: Eerdmans, 1964), vol. 1, pp. 88–115.

58. The classic work is that of Rudolf Otto, *The Idea of the Holy: An Inquiry into the Non-Rational Factor in the Idea of the Divine and Its Relation to the Rational* (1931), trans. John H. Harvey, 2nd ed. (New York: Oxford University Press, 1950).

59. This is the famous sixth thesis of Marx against Feuerbach.

60. See A. M. Besnard, *Le mystère du nom* (Paris, 1962); van den Bussche, *Understanding the Lord's Prayer*, pp. 65–75; J. Dupont in *Dictionnaire de la Bible*, Supp., vol. 6, "*nom*," pp. 514–41.

61. Origen, *De oratione*, P.G. 11, 489–549, translation by Hamman, *Le Pater expliqué*, p. 59.

62. See the beautiful text of 1 Cor. 6:9–11, where it says that we have

been dedicated to God and justified through the name of the Lord Jesus and the Spirit of our God.

63. For the Bible everything is in relation to the Holy One (God) and becomes holy through participation: the nation, the temple, sacred objects (holy things), the land, persons, etc. This holiness is never considered in itself outside this bond with God, the unique font of all holiness: *tu solus sanctus!*

64. See the reflections of Alves, *O enigma da religião.*

65. See the reflections and bibliography in Leonardo Boff, *A ressurreição de Cristo, a nossa ressurreição na morte* (Petrópolis: Vozes, 1976) and *Vida para além da morte: O presente—seu futuro, sua festa, sua contestação* (Petrópolis: Vozes, 1978), pp. 17–26.

66. W. Knörzer, *Reich Gottes, Traum, Hoffnung, Wirklichkeit* (Stuttgart, 1970); Walter Nigg, *Das ewige Reich: Geschichte einer Hoffnung* (Munich-Hamburg, 1967), which traces the history of the idea of the kingdom of God along the trajectory of the centuries.

67. See Lohmeyer, *The Lord's Prayer,* pp. 95–100; Jeremias, *New Testament Theology,* pp. 108–21.

68. Jeremias, *New Testament Theology,* p. 102.

69. See Jean Dupont, *Les béatitudes,* II, *La bonne nouvelle* (Bruges: Abbey of Saint André, 1958; Paris, 1969); E. Semain, "Manifesto de libertação: O discurso-programa de Nazaré (Luke 4:16–21)," *REB* 34 (1974): 261–81, esp. 279–80.

70. Origen, *De oratione,* P.G. 11, 489–549; translation in Hamman, *Le Pater expliqué,* p. 61.

71. See the letter of Marx, Feb. 16, 1881, to Vera Zassoulitch, cited by M. Godelier, "Marxisme, anthropologie, et religion," *Epistémologie et marxisme* (Paris, 1972), pp. 223–24.

72. St. Augustine, *Sermo 56,* 4–14, P.L. 39, 379–386; translation in Hamman, *Le Pater expliqué,* p. 139.

73. Tertullian, *De oratione,* P.L. 1, 1153–1165; translation in Hamman, *Le Pater expliqué,* p. 20.

74. Cyril of Jerusalem, *Catequeses mistagogicas,* P.G. 33, 1117–24; translation in Hamman, *Le Pater expliqué,* p. 107.

75. For a detailed exegesis of this supplication, see the bibliography referred to in previous chapters, as also Raymond E. Brown and others in the Bibliography.

76. See Leonardo Boff, *Paixão de Cristo, paixão do mundo* (Petrópolis: Vozes, 1978), pp. 28–29.

77. This is the interpretation preferred by the fathers of the church in their explanations of the Lord's Prayer. See Hamman, *Le Pater expliqué.*

78. See statements of these authors in Lohmeyer, *The Lord's Prayer*, p. 116, and Heiler, *Prayer*, pp. 89–93.

79. Tertullian, in his commentary (P.L. 1, 1153–65), says, "In this petition we warn ourselves to have patience"; Cyprian declares, "It is not that God should do what we want, but that we should do what God wants" (*De oratione dominica*, P.L. 4, 521–38); see Hamman, *Le Pater expliqué*, pp. 19 and 33.

80. Origen, *De oratione*, P.G. 11, 489–549, translation in Hamman, *Le Pater expliqué*, p. 68.

81. The commentaries of the church fathers prefer the spiritual interpretation of this petition, with the exception of Theodore of Mopsuestia. The bread refers immediately to Jesus Christ and the Eucharist; for this see Hamman, *Le Pater expliqué*. As for later commentaries, see the collection of texts where the spiritual interpretation predominates: K. Becker and M. Peter, *Das heilige Vater-unser: Ein Werkbuch* (Freiburg: Herder, 1951), pp. 224–50.

82. See the reflections of Gerhart Ebeling, *Vom Gebet: Predichte über das Unser-Vater* (Tübingen: Mohn, 1963); Eng., *On Prayer: The Lord's Prayer in Today's World*, trans. James W. Leiten (Philadelphia: Fortress, n.d.).

83. See the pertinent reflections of Karl Barth, *Das Vater-unser* (Zurich, 1965), pp. 76–79.

84. *Magistri Echardi Tractatus super oratione dominica*, in *Werke* V/1–2, ed. E. Seeberg, pp. 103–28; this citation, p. 120.

85. On this word (*epiousios*) there are innumerable studies. We cite only the more recent: F. M. Braun, "Le pain dont nous avons besoin (Mt 6;1, Lc 11,3)," *Nouvelle Revue Théologique* 110 (1978): 559–68; W. Rordorf, "Le 'pain quotidien' (Math 6, 11) dans l'histoire de l'exégèse," *Didaskalia* (Journal of the Faculty of Theology of Lisbon) 6 (1976): 221–25.

86. Origen, *De oratione* 27, 7, P.G. 11, 509c.

87. See F. Preisigke, *Sammelbuch griechischer Urkunden aus Aegypten* (Strasburg, 1915), I, 5224. This papyrus has vanished; its editor, Sayce, as Raymond E. Brown informs us ("The Pater Noster as an Eschatological Prayer," *Theological Studies* 22 [1961]: 175–208; here p. 195, note 86), was not particularly meticulous. In this papyrus the word *epious* appears, probably as an abbreviation of *epiousion*, in the context of a list of distributions, signifying "what is necessary for one day," "wages of one day," "a day's rations."

88. St. Jerome, *Comm. in Matthvi,11*, P.L. 36, 43. Decidedly against this view is the study of P. Grelot, "La quatriéme demande du Pater et son arriére-plan sémitique," *New Testament Studies* 25 (1979): 299–314.

89. H. Bourgoin, "Epioúsios expliqué par la notion de préfixe," *Biblica* 60 (1979): 91-96.

90. Classic works go back to this interpretation, in accord with Jeremias, *The Prayers of Jesus*, pp. 100-102, and Lohmeyer, *The Lord's Prayer*, pp. 134-59, as also Brown, "The Pater Noster," *Theological Studies* 22, note 7.

91. See Leonardo Boff, *Jesus Cristo Libertador*, 7th ed. (Petrópolis: Vozes, 1979); Eng., *Jesus Christ Liberator: A Critical Christology for Our Time*, trans. Patrick Hughes (Maryknoll, N.Y.: Orbis, 1978); and *Paixão de Cristo, paixão do mundo*, 2nd ed. (Petrópolis: Vozes, 1977).

92. This point is well explored in Romano Guardini's commentary on the Lord's Prayer, *Das Gebet des Herrn* (Mainz: Grünewald, 1934); Eng., *The Lord's Prayer*, trans. Isabel McHugh (New York: Pantheon, 1958), pp. 17-25, 69-78; and that by Grelot in the article cited in note 88.

93. Van den Bussche, *Understanding the Lord's Prayer*, pp. 116-17.

94. See the excellent reflections of Origen in regard to this point, *De oratione*, P.G. 11, 489-549, in the translation by Hamman, *Le Pater expliqué*, pp. 81-84.

95. See A. Moser, "Pecado, culpa e psicanálise," *REB* 35 (1975): 5-36.

96. Clodovis Boff, "Pecado social," *REB* 37 (1977): 675-701.

97. See L. Goppelt, *Teología do Novo Testamento* (São Leopoldo-Petrópolis, 1976), p. 154.

98. A detailed analysis of the parables of mercy and pardon will be found in Joachim Jeremias, *Die Gleichnisse Jesu* (Munich-Hamburg, 1966), pp. 84-99; Eng., *The Parables of Jesus*, trans. S. H. Hooke (New York: Scribner's, 1963), pp. 124-46.

99. See Lohmeyer, *The Lord's Prayer*, pp. 186-90.

100. Enrique Dussel, *El humanismo semita* (Buenos Aires, 1969); H. W. Wolff, *Antropología do Antigo Testamento* (São Paulo, 1977), I, 2; Leonardo Boff, "Aprendendo a ser: Momentos da antropología cristã," *Grande Sinal* 32 (1978): 323-34.

101. See Ignace de la Potterie and Stanislas Lyonnet, *La vie selon l'esprit: Condition du chrétien* (Paris: Cerf, 1965); Eng., *The Christian Lives by the Spirit* (Staten Island: Society of St. Paul, 1971), pp. 156-193.

102. J. B. Libânio, *Pecado e opção fundamental* (Petrópolis: Vozes, 1975), pp. 42-87.

103. For this whole problematic, see Leonardo Boff, "O pecado original: Discussão antiga e moderna e pistas de equacionamento," *Grande Sinal* 29 (1975): 109-33, and A. Villalmonte, *El Pecado Original* (Salamanca, 1978).

104. See J. Kamp, *Souffrance de Dieu, vie du monde* (Paris: Caster-

man, 1971), pp. 47–92; Leonardo Boff, *Teología do cativeiro e da libertação* (Lisbon: Multinova, 1976), pp. 113–34.

105. See Edward Schillebeeckx, "Jesus e o fracasso na vida humana," *Concilium* 113 (1976): 88–99.

106. Van den Bussche, *Understanding the Lord's Prayer*, p. 134; Lohmeyer, *The Lord's Prayer*, pp. 195–208.

107. The original sense of the petition was situated within an apocalyptico-eschatological horizon; see Brown, "The Pater Noster as an Eschatological Prayer," *Theological Studies* 22 (1961): 204–8; a very lucid study is that of K. Kuhn, "Jesus in Gethsemani," *Evangelische Theologie* 12 (1952): 260–85.

108. See Jean Piaget, *Le Structuralisme* (Paris: Presses Universitaires de France, 1968), pp. 5–16; Eng., *Structuralism*, trans. Cheminah Maschler (New York: Basic Books, 1970; Harper Torchbooks, 1971).

109. See E. Támez, S. Trinidad, et al., *Capitalismo: violencia y antivida*, 2 vols. (San José, Costa Rica: DEI, 1978).

110. See Clodovis Boff, *Os sinais dos tempos: Pautas de leitura* (São Paulo, 1979), which is a very important work on this theme.

111. Piet Schoonenberg, "O pecado do mundo," *Mysterium Salutis* II/3 (Petrópolis: Vozes, 1972), p. 306.

112. Boff, "O pecado original," pp. 109–33.

113. See Sabourin, *Il vangelo di Matteo*, pp. 448–50; J. Schmid, *Das Evangelium nach Mattäus*, Regensburger Neues Testament, vol. 1 (Regensberg, 1965), pp. 133–35; Lohmeyer, *The Lord's Prayer*, pp. 209–17. In Greek, the phrase is *apo tou ponerou*; the noun (*ponerou*) is in the genitive case; we do not know morphologically whether the nominative is neuter (*poneron*) or masculine (*poneros*). In the first case it would signify iniquity or evil; in the second, the evil one. Probably the masculine (*poneros*) is intended, because of the definite article (*tou*) that precedes it. The neuter normally appears without the article. Luke omits this petition; it is in Matthew's version. The Greek fathers, sensitive to the nuances of their language, interpret this in the sense of the evil one (masculine). The Latin fathers, on the contrary—because in Latin the article does not exist—take it in the sense of iniquity, evil (neuter)—*libera nos a malo*.

114. On this question, see the two basic positions: Christian Duquoc, "Satan—symbole ou réalité," *Lumière et Vie* 78 (1966); 99–105; Herbert Haag, *El diablo, un fantasma* (Barcelona: Herder, 1973), and Joseph Ratzinger, "Abschied vom Teufel?" in *Dogma und Verkündigung* (Munich, 1973), pp. 225–34.

115. Rudolf Schnackenburg, "Der Sinn der Versuchung Jesu bei den

Synoptikern," in *Schriften zum Neuen Testament* (Munich, 1971), p. 127.

116. See the fundamental work of Herbert Haag in collaboration with other exegetes and theologians, *El diablo: Su existencia como problema* (Barcelona: Herder, 1978).

117. See Van der Leeuw, *Religion in Essence and Manifestation*, vol. 1, chaps. 15, 16, and 19.

118. See J. Ernst, *Die eschatologischen Gegenspieler in den Schriften des Neuen Testaments* (Regensburg, 1967), pp. 221–40.

119. A systematic and rigorously exegetical treatment of this can be found in Haag, "Jesús y la realidad del mal," *El diablo: Su existencia*, pp. 199–246.

120. Jeremias, "Overcoming the Rule of Satan," in *New Testament Theology*, pp. 85–96.

121. See Haag, *El diablo: Su existencia*, p. 244.

122. See *Reallexikon für Antike und Christentum*, vol. 8 (1972), p. 303, *"Freiheit."*

123. See F. Reiniker, "Amen," in *Lexikon zur Bibel* (1960), pp. 67–68.

124. For an exegesis of these passages, see H. Schlier, "Amen," in *Theologisches Wörterbuch*, vol. 1, pp. 339–43; Eng., *Theological Dictionary*, vol. 1, pp. 335–38.

Bibliography

Barth, Karl. *Das Vater-unser.* Zurich, 1965.

Bourgoin, H. "Epiousios expliqué par la notion du préfixe." *Biblica* 60 (1979): 91–96.

Braun, F.-M. "Le pain dont nous avons besoin (Mt 6, 11; Lc 11, 3)." *Nouvelle Revue Théologique* 110 (1978): 559–68.

Brown, Raymond E. "The Pater Noster as an Eschatological Prayer." *Theological Studies* 22 (1961): 175–208.

Bussche, H. van den. *Le Notre Père.* Brussels, 1960; Eng., *Understanding the Lord's Prayer.* Trans. Charles Schaldenbrand. New York: Sheed & Ward, 1963.

Carmignac, J. *Recherches sur le "Notre Père."* Paris, 1969.

Dalman, G. *Die Worte Jesu.* Vol. 1. Darmstadt, 1965, pp. 283–365.

Díaz, Alonso, "El problema literario del Padre Nuestro." *Estudios Bíblicos* 18 (1959): 63–75.

Dibelius, Oscar. *Das Vater-unser: Umrisse zu einer Geschichte des Gebets in der alten und mittleren Kirche.* Giessen, 1903.

Didaskalia 6 (1976). This whole issue is devoted to the Lord's Prayer in Portuguese literature and in the mystics in Portugal.

Ebeling, Gerhart. *Vom Gebet: Predichte über das Unser-Vater.* Tübingen: Mohn, 1963; Eng., *On Prayer: The Lord's Prayer in Today's World.* Trans. James Leiten. Philadelphia: Fortress, n.d.

Grelot, P. "La quatrième demande du Pater et son arrière-plan sémitique." *New Testament Studies* 25 (1979): 299–314.

Guardini, Romano. *Das Gebet des Herrn.* Mainz: Grunewald, 1934; Eng., *The Lord's Prayer.* Trans. Isabel McHugh. New York: Pantheon, 1958.

Hamman, Adalbert. "La prière du Seigneur." In *La Prière*, vol. 1. Tournaise: Desclée, 1959.

———. *Le Pater expliqué par les Pères.* Paris: Ed. Franciscaines, 1952.

Hensler, J. *Das Vater-unser*. N.T. Abhandlungen 4/5, 1914.

Jeremias, Joachim. *Abba: Studien zur neutestmentlichen Theologie und Zeitgeschichte*. Göttingen; Vandenhoeck & Ruprecht, 1966; Eng., Chapters 1, 2, and 4 of *Abba, The Prayers of Jesus*. Philadelphia: Fortress, 1978.

Kuss, Otto. "Das Vater-unser." In *Auslegung und Verkündigung*, vol 2. Regensburg, 1967.

Leaney, R. "The Lucan Text of the Lord's Prayer." *New Testament* 1 (1956): 103–11.

Lohmeyer, Ernst. *Das Vater-unser*. Zurich: Vandenhoeck & Ruprecht, 1952.

Lotz, J. *Wenn ihr heute Vater-unser betet*. Fribourg, 1978.

Manson, T.W. "The Lord's Prayer." *Bulletin of the John Rylands Library* 38 (Manchester, 1955/1956): 436–48.

Marchel, W. *Abba, Père: La prière du Christ et des chrétiens*. Rome, 1963.

———. *Dieu-Père dans le nouveau Testament*. Paris: Cerf, 1966.

Sabourin, L. *Il vangelo di Matteo: Teologia e Esegesi*. Rome, 1976.

Schmidt, J. *Das Evangelium nach Mattäus*, Regensburger Neues Testament, vol. 1. Regensburg, 1965, pp. 344–62.

Schneider, R. *Das Vater-unser*. Fribourg, 1978.

Schürmann, H. *Das Gebet des Herrn*. Fribourg, 1958.

Schwartz, G. "Matthäus VI. 9–13/Lukas XI. 2–4: Emendation und Räckübersetzung." *New Testament Studies* 15 (1969): 233–47.

Soiron, T. *Die Bergpredigt Jesu*. Fribourg, 1941, pp. 314–70.

Vögtle, A. "Der 'eschatologische' Bezug der Wir-Bitten des Vater-unsers." In *Jesus und Paulus*, Festschrift für W.G. Kümmel. Göttingen, 1975, pp. 344–62.

Wulf, F. *Vater-unser im Himmel*. Zurich-Würzburg, 1969.

Index of Scriptural References

Compiled by Thomas P. Fenton

OLD TESTAMENT

NEW TESTAMENT